THE CARTOON GUIDE TO
THE CONSTITUTION OF THE UNITED STATES

THE CARTOON GUIDE TO
The Constitution of the United States

Eric Lurio

BARNES & NOBLE BOOKS
A DIVISION OF HARPER & ROW, PUBLISHERS
New York, Cambridge, Philadelphia
San Francisco, Washington, London, Mexico City
São Paulo, Singapore, Sydney

To my mother, Marilyn Lurio,
and to Maurice and Frone Eisenstadt
(and Nancy T. and all 16 Marks)

FIRST EDITION

Contents

PART ONE

WHY WE NEEDED A CONSTITUTION IN THE FIRST PLACE

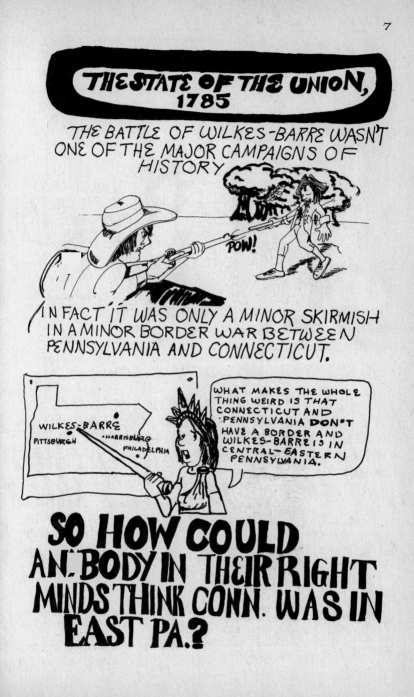

THE PROBLEM WAS THE TREATY OF PARIS (1783). UNDER ITS PROVISIONS, GREAT BRITAIN CEDED ALMOST ALL ITS LANDS SOUTH OF THE GREAT LAKES AND EAST OF THE MISSISSIPPI RIVER TO A COUNTRY CALLED "THE UNITED STATES OF AMERICA."

WHAT THERE **WAS** WAS THE 2ND CONTINENTAL CONGRESS.

IT WAS SET UP IN 1775 TO COORDINATE THE REVOLUTIONARY WAR, WHICH WAS NOW OVER. SO IT REALLY HAD NOTHING TO DO ANYMORE. BUT IT LINGERED ON AS SORT OF A "LEAGUE OF FRIENDSHIP" UNDER A PITIFULLY WEAK CHARTER CALLED "THE ARTICLES OF CONFEDERATION."

AMONG THE MANY POWERS THAT THE ARTICLES **DIDN'T** CONFER ON CONGRESS WAS THE ABILITY TO ADMINISTER THE WESTERN LANDS CEDED IN 1783.

MINE! NO MINE! MINE

SO IT WAS EVERY STATE FOR ITSELF!

THE WILKES-BARRE SITUATION WAS ONLY SYMPTOMATIC (IN FACT CONNECTICUT WAS WILLING TO CEDE WILKES-BARRE TO CONGRESS IF PENNSYLVANIA AGREED. BUT CONGRESS REFUSED).

ASIDE FROM WILKES-BARRE, PENNSYLVANIA CLAIMED BUFFALO, NEW YORK. VIRGINIA CLAIMED OHIO, WHICH WAS ALSO CLAIMED BY MASSACHUSETTS & CON-NECTICUT. KENTUCKY (CLAIMED BY NEW YORK & VIRGINIA) WAS THINKING OF BECOMING A SPANISH SATELLITE. NORTH CAROLINA WAS AT WAR WITH SOMETHING CALLED THE "STATE OF FRANKLIN," & NEW YORK HAD IT IN FOR VERMONT (AND WE DIDN'T EVEN MENTION INDIAN ATTACKS).

AND TO TOP IT OFF, THERE WAS ONE HECK OF A DEPRESSION GOING ON...

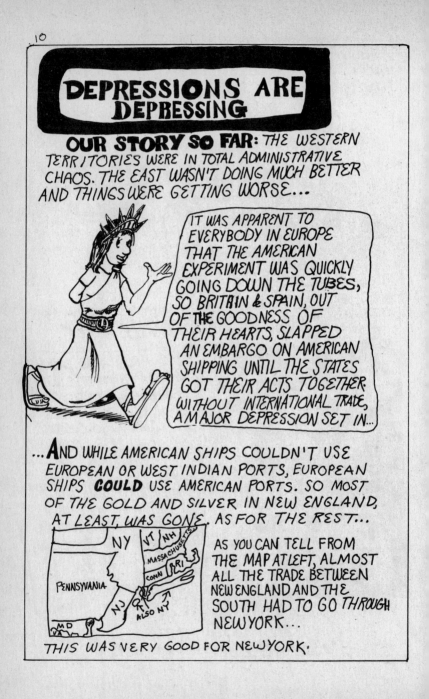

DEPRESSIONS ARE DEPRESSING

OUR STORY SO FAR: THE WESTERN TERRITORIES WERE IN TOTAL ADMINISTRATIVE CHAOS. THE EAST WASN'T DOING MUCH BETTER AND THINGS WERE GETTING WORSE...

IT WAS APPARENT TO EVERYBODY IN EUROPE THAT THE AMERICAN EXPERIMENT WAS QUICKLY GOING DOWN THE TUBES, SO BRITAIN & SPAIN, OUT OF THE GOODNESS OF THEIR HEARTS, SLAPPED AN EMBARGO ON AMERICAN SHIPPING UNTIL THE STATES GOT THEIR ACTS TOGETHER. WITHOUT INTERNATIONAL TRADE, A MAJOR DEPRESSION SET IN...

...AND WHILE AMERICAN SHIPS COULDN'T USE EUROPEAN OR WEST INDIAN PORTS, EUROPEAN SHIPS **COULD** USE AMERICAN PORTS. SO MOST OF THE GOLD AND SILVER IN NEW ENGLAND, AT *LEAST*, WAS GONE. AS FOR THE REST...

NY VT NH
MASSACHUSETTS
CONN RI
PENNSYLVANIA
NJ
ALSO NY
MD

AS YOU CAN TELL FROM THE MAP AT LEFT, ALMOST ALL THE TRADE BETWEEN NEW ENGLAND AND THE SOUTH HAD TO GO THROUGH NEW YORK...

THIS WAS VERY GOOD FOR NEW YORK.

RhODE ISLAND WAS ABOUT TO DEFAULT ON ITS MYRIAD DEBTS. BUT THEN IT FOUND A NIFTY SOLUTION.

PAPER MONEY!

NOWADAYS, PAPER MONEY IS THE NORMAL, IF NOT ESSENTIAL, WAY OF DOING BUSINESS. BUT IN 1786 IT WAS A DIFFERENT STORY...

CONGRESS USED PAPER MONEY TO PAY THE TROOPS DURING THE REVOLUTION THESE WERE I.O.U.'S PAYABLE AFTER THE WAR.

WHERE'S MY MONEY?

YOU'RE HOLDING IT.

THE PROMISE WAS PROMPTLY WELSHED ON.

IN THE SPRING OF 1786 RHODE ISLAND PASSED A PAPER MONEY ACT...

THIS IS $20 aum

MONEY FOR EVERYBODY!

RHODE ISLAND ISSUED NOTES BACKED IN NOTHING. THE ACT HAD ENFORCEMENT PROVISIONS...

THEY WORKED LIKE THIS:

FARMER BROWN WOULD TAKE OUT A LONG-TERM, LOW-INTEREST MORTGAGE FROM THE STATE

HERE YA GO

IN PAPER MONEY.

HE WOULD THEN ATTEMPT TO PAY HIS CREDITORS

GO AWAY

BUT IT'S YOURS!

BUT NOBODY WOULD TAKE IT.

WHY?

BECAUSE IT ISN'T BACKED BY ANYTHING! GOLD AND SILVER HAVE VALUE, PAPER DOESN'T. BESIDES, NOBODY ELSE WILL TAKE IT!

IF A CREDITOR REFUSED TO TAKE THE "SHINPLASTERS," AS THEY WERE CALLED, FARMER BROWN COULD DEPOSIT HIS MONEY AT THE LOCAL COURTHOUSE, PUT AN AD IN THE LOCAL PAPER, WAIT 3 WEEKS...

KNOW YE YOUR MONEY'S AT THE COURT-HOUSE —F. BROWN

AND IF THE CREDITOR DIDN'T PICK IT UP, THE DEBT WAS CANCELED!

THIS IS FUN!

BY THE TIME EVERYBODY FIGURED OUT WHAT WAS GOING ON, THE LOWER CLASSES WERE OUT OF DEBT! THE RHODE ISLAND GOVERNMENT WOULD USE SHINPLASTERS TO PAY ITS FOREIGN DEBTS AS WELL. THIS GOT EVERYBODY IN THE WORLD MAD AT THE STATE

ROGUE ISLAND! —"

(INCLUDING NORTH CAROLINA, WHICH WAS DOING PRETTY MUCH THE SAME THING).

GEORGE WASHINGTON BUILDS A CANAL (SORT OF)

ONE OF THE STRANGER BITS OF HISTORY IS HOW GEORGE WASHINGTON WOULD POP UP AT THE MOST OPPORTUNE MOMENTS...

FOUNDING FATHER #2
GEORGE WASHINGTON (1732-1799)

STARTED THE FRENCH AND INDIAN WAR IN 1754. COMMANDER-IN-CHIEF OF THE U.S.A. 1775-1783 NOW RETIRED

OL' GEORGE

WASHINGTON SPENT MOST OF HIS RETIREMENT TRAMPING OUT IN THE BACKWOODS OF WHAT IS NOW KENTUCKY AND OHIO.

IT WAS HERE THAT HE CAME UP WITH A NIFTY IDEA TO CONNECT LAKE ERIE WITH THE POTOMAC RIVER.

ALL WE HAFTA DO IS CONNECT THIS RIVER HERE WITH THAT RIVER THERE. WE'LL MAKE MILLIONS!

LAKE ERIE

VIRGINIA

MD.

ZZ

BUT A PROJECT ON SUCH A LARGE SCALE NEEDED A HUGE AMOUNT OF MONEY, WHICH THE GENERAL DIDN'T HAVE (HE WAS ALMOST BANKRUPT). STATE FUNDING WAS IMPERATIVE.

BUT NOT FORTHCOMING...

WE'D LIKE TO HELP YOU, GENERAL, BUT MARYLAND CONTROLS THE POTOMAC.

SO WE'LL GIVE 'EM A CUT.

UH, YEAH

BUT THE GENERAL WOULD NOT BE DETERRED! HE AND HIS SUPPORTERS GOT THE VA. HOUSE OF DELEGATES TO INVITE COMMISSIONERS FROM MARYLAND TO DISCUSS THE CANAL PROJECT.

THE MARYLAND LEGISLATURE SUGGESTED THAT THE MEETING TAKE PLACE IN ALEXANDRIA, VA. IN MARCH, 1785.

THEY RECEIVED NO REPLY, AND ASSUMED THAT THE TIME & PLACE HAD BEEN ACCEPTED.

BUT VA. GOV. PATRICK ("GIVE ME LIBERTY OR GIVE ME DEATH") HENRY HAD, IN FACT, DESTROYED THE LETTER.

HEE HEE HEE

SO WHEN THE MARYLAND DELEGATION ARRIVED IN ALEXANDRIA, THE VIRGINIA DELEGATION WAS NOWHERE TO BE FOUND...

DON'T LOOK AT ME! I DIDN'T LOSE 'EM

SO THEY STARTED LOOKING...

AND AFTER A WHILE, THEY FOUND...

FOUNDING FATHER #3

GEORGE MASON
(1726-1792)
MEMBER OF VA. COLONIAL HOUSE OF BURGESSES AND ESTEEMED JUDGE. AUTHOR OF THE VIRGINIA BILL OF RIGHTS.

SORRY, GUYS, I DIDN'T KNOW!

MASON SET UP A QUICKIE INVESTIGATION TO FIND OUT WHAT HAPPENED, AND BEGAN TO PULL STRINGS TO PUT THE CONFERENCE BACK ON TRACK.

PATRICK HENRY FEIGNED IGNORANCE.

CONFERENCE? WHAT CONFERENCE?

WASHINGTON WAS BOILING MAD.

THAT @#$! HENRY!

AS MASON ROUNDED UP THE OTHER VIRGINIA COMMISSIONERS, WASHINGTON ENTERTAINED THE MARYLANDERS AT HIS ESTATE. THE VIRGINIANS WENT THERE TOO, AND THE GET-TOGETHER HAS SINCE BEEN CALLED...

THE MT. VERNON CONFERENCE

WORK ON THE POTOMAC CANAL TREATY WENT QUICK AND EASY. THE DELEGATES WERE ENTHUSIASTIC.

THIS IS FUN! LET'S DO IT AGAIN!

IN FACT, ONE OF THE CONFEREES, SAMUEL CHASE (LATER, ON THE SUPREME COURT), MANAGED TO GET THE MARYLAND LEGISLATURE TO PROPOSE AN AN EXPANDED PROJECT.

WE COULD ADD PENNSYLVANIA AND DELAWARE TO THE SCHEME AND BUILD A CANAL BETWEEN CHESAPEAKE AND DELAWARE BAYS.

VIRGINIA WENT MARYLAND ONE BETTER.

LET'S INVITE ALL THIRTEEN STATES AND HAVE A GENERAL CONFERENCE ON EVERYTHING!

WHAT ABOUT FRANKLIN?

THAT DOESN'T COUNT.

IT WAS AGREED THAT THE CONFERENCE WOULD TAKE PLACE IN ANNAPOLIS, MARYLAND, IN THE FALL OF 1786. THINGS WERE LOOKING UP.

THEN DISASTER STRUCK!

SHAYS' REBELLION

PART ONE:
TAXATION **WITH** REPRESENTATION AIN'T SO GOOD EITHER.

THE DISASTER WAS A CIVIL WAR IN MASSACHUSETTS! ...ACCORDING TO KARL MARX (WHO ON RARE OCCASIONS **WAS** RIGHT) THE AMERICAN REVOLUTION WAS A "BOURGEOIS" REVOLUTION, THE RICH AND MIDDLE CLASSES OVERTHROWING THE FEUDAL NOBILITY (A.K.A. KING GEORGE III).

DURING THE NEXT PHASE, THE RICH AND UPPER-MIDDLE CLASS WOULD DISENFRANCHISE THE PEASANTS AND PROLETARIAT (WHICH DIDN'T EXIST IN 1786) AND STEAL THEIR LAND AND PROPERTY...

THIS DESCRIPTION FIT THE MASSACHUSETTS SITUATION TO A TEE!

GET ME OUT!

THE MASS. CONSTITUTION OF 1780 SEVERELY LIMITED THE FRANCHISE. YOU HAD TO OWN REAL ESTATE IN ORDER TO VOTE FOR THE LOWER HOUSE OF THE GENERAL COURT (LEGISLATURE).

ANYBODY WHO DOESN'T OWN LAND IS **TOO STUPID** TO VOTE!

FOUNDING FATHER #1

JOHN ADAMS
(1735-1826)
REVOLUTIONARY, DIPLOMAT, AND PRINCIPAL AUTHOR OF THE 1780 MASSACHUSETTS CONSTITUTION.

YOU HAD TO BE WEALTHY TO VOTE IN SENATORIAL ELECTIONS OR FOR GOVERNOR...

...AND TO HOLD OFFICE, YOU HAD TO BE

IT'S MINE! MINE! ALL MINE!

PERFECT SENATORIAL MATERIAL

FILTHY, STINKING RICH!

BUT WORST OF ALL, YOU HAD TO PAY A LARGE FEE TO BE ALLOWED TO DEFEND YOURSELF IN COURT.

WHERE'S YOUR FEE?

NO FEE, EH? **THEN YOU MUST BE GUILTY**

I CAN'T AFFORD IT, YOUR HONOR.

THE SITUATION WAS INTOLERABLE. MASS MEETINGS WERE HELD IN MOST TOWNS AND VILLAGES IN WESTERN MASSACHUSETTS.

THEY HAD RISEN UP AGAINST TYRANNY BEFORE; THEY WOULD DO IT AGAIN!

IN THE SUMMER OF 1786, THE MASSACHUSETTS SUPERIOR JUDICIAL WAS GOING TO MEET AND TAKE AWAY LAND FROM POOR FARMERS FOUR MONTHS EARLY* AND TAKE FOOD OUT OF THE MOUTHS OF WIDOWS AND ORPHANS.

BUT THEY DIDN'T COUNT ON LUKE DAY AND OVER A THOUSAND MINUTEMEN.

THE LOCAL MILITIA, INSTEAD OF DEFENDING THE JUDGES, JOINED THE REVOLT.

IN GREAT BARRINGTON, ONE JUDGE WANTED TO SEE WHO THE "TRAITORS" WERE.

LOYALISTS TO THE LEFT, TRAITORS TO THE RIGHT!

OUT OF 1000 MILITIAMEN ONLY 200 WERE "LOYAL!"

THE MOVEMENT SPREAD EAST TOWARD BOSTON.

GREAT BARRINGTON

BOSTON

THE SPIRIT OF '76 LIVED ON!

THIS NEW REVOLUTION WAS BASED ON THREE REASONABLE DEMANDS:

1. JUDICIAL COURT REFORM
2. ABOLITION OF THE SENATE
AND 3. AN ISSUE OF PAPER MONEY À LA RHODE ISLAND.

* THE LOANS WEREN'T DUE UNTIL OCTOBER, WHEN THE HARVEST WAS IN, AND IF THE BANKS FORECLOSED EARLY, THEY COULD GET THE CROPS, TOO.

BUT GOVERNOR JAMES BOWDOIN HAD ANOTHER NAME FOR THIS GLORIOUS REVOLUTION...

TREASON!

BOWDOIN THEN ASKED FEDERAL SECRETARY OF WAR HENRY KNOX FOR TROOPS.

KNOX (WHO WAS IN BOSTON AT THE TIME) WAS SYMPATHETIC, BUT THE ANSWER WAS

NO

HE WOULD LATER CHANGE HIS MIND AND RAISE 1300 TROOPS, BY WHICH TIME THE MESS WAS OVER

THE REBELS, UNDER DANIEL SHAYS, WERE PREPARING TO MARCH ON BOSTON.

DANIEL SHAYS 1747-1825

AND THAT'S WHERE IT STOOD WHEN THE DELEGATES MET AT THE ANNAPOLIS CONVENTION

SOME OLD PATRIOTS VIOLENTLY DENOUNCED THE EXACT SAME TACTICS THEY THEMSELVES USED 10 YEARS BEFORE.

WE'LL BE SEEING MORE OF THAT.

MEANWHILE, IN RHODE ISLAND...

THE RHODE ISLAND SUPREME COURT MADE A SURPRISE DECISION.

PAPER MONEY IS UNCONSTITUTIONAL

SO THE RHODE ISLAND LEGISLATURE DECLARED THE COURT UNCONSTITUTIONAL

RHODE ISLAND HAD NO CONSTITUTION IN 1786

IN MASSACHUSETTS, THINGS WERE GETTING WORSE.

SHAYS' REBELLION

PART TWO: NOTHING FAILS LIKE FAILURE!

JAN. 1787: DANIEL SHAYS LEADS 1500 REBELS TO ATTACK THE ARSENAL AT SPRINGFIELD.

WHICH GEN. WILLIAM SHEPHERD AND 600 MILITIA STAND READY TO DEFEND.

MOST OF THE REBELS' DEMANDS WERE MET. PARDONS WERE OFFERED.

BUT THEY KEPT ON COMING.

SHEPHERD DIDN'T WANT VIOLENCE.

STOP OR WE'LL SHOOT

HE WARNED.

DESPITE ITS FAILURE, SHAYS' REBELLION
SCARED THE HECK OUT OF EVERYBODY.
THE LEGISLATURES TOOK ACTION.

BUT CONGRESS COULDN'T STOMACH THE
IDEA OF AN ILLEGAL CONVENTION.

EXCEPT THIS ONE WAS SUPPOSED TO MAKE
A FEW AMENDMENTS. ALL WAS SET. THE
SUMMER WOULD BE AMAZING!

PART TWO

THE GREAT CONVENTION OF 1787

30

ARRIVAL

OUR STORY SO FAR: THE BIG SHOW STARTS MAY FOURTEENTH.

THE FIRST DELEGATION TO ARRIVE IN PHILADELPHIA WAS PENNSYLVANIA'S.

HOME SWEET HOME

THAT'S BECAUSE WE ALL LIVE HERE.

BUT THE NEXT DELEGATION TO ARRIVE WAS REALLY IMPORTANT.

ON MAY 3, 1787, THE FIRST OUT-OF-TOWNER ARRIVED IN PHILLY. WE MET HIM SIX PAGES BACK.

FOUNDING FATHER #*

JAMES MADISON JR.

(1751-1836) "JEMMY" TO HIS FRIENDS, HE WAS A PROFESSIONAL POLITICIAN ALL HIS LIFE. HE HELPED WRITE VIRGINIA'S FIRST CONSTITUTION.

* AWW, TO HECK WITH IT.

THE OFFICIAL REASON JEMMY MADISON ARRIVED EARLY WAS TO CONFIRM THE VIRGINIA DELEGATION'S HOTEL RESERVATIONS. BUT IN REALITY HE WISHED TO COLLECT HIS THOUGHTS...

...SO WITH PEN IN HAND, AND HIS FAVORITE PHILOSOPHERS BY HIS SIDE, OUR HERO BEGINS TO COMPOSE A NATION.

IF MEN WERE ANGELS, NO GOVERNMENT WOULD BE NECESSARY...

AND IF ANGELS WERE TO GOVERN MEN, NO EXTERNAL OR INTERNAL CONTROLS WOULD BE NECESSARY...

SO THE QUESTION IS: HOW TO MAKE GOVERNMENT EFFECTIVE WHILE KEEPING THE GOVERNORS HONEST AT THE SAME TIME.

BUT THAT'S THE TROUBLE. YOU CAN NEVER FIND A DECENT ANGEL WHEN YOU NEED ONE!

HMMM...

WHAT WE NEED IS A SERIES OF CHECKS AND BALANCES...

32

BY THE 25ᵗʰ ENOUGH DELEGATIONS HAD SHOWN UP TO CONSTITUTE A QUORUM.

OUR CAST, THE RULES & OTHER SUNDRIES

THE FIRST PERSON TO FORMALLY SPEAK WAS ROBERT MORRIS.

THE NEXT ORDER OF BUSINESS WAS TO READ THE CREDENTIALS OF THE SEVERAL DELEGATIONS.

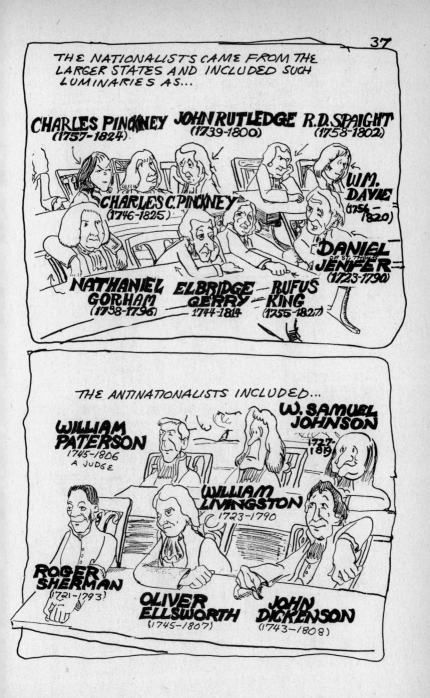

3. WE CAN VOTE AS MANY TIMES AS WE LIKE ON ANY SUBJECT. IF SOMEBODY HAS A BETTER IDEA ON A SUBJECT ALREADY VOTED ON, WE DON'T WANT TO LOSE IT.
4. ALL SPEECHES WILL BE ADDRESSED TO THE PRESIDENT. MAINLY TO PRESERVE DECORUM AND AVOID FISTFIGHTS.
5. NO TALKING, CARD PLAYING OR READING OF NEWSPAPERS. THIS IS TOO IMPORTANT FOR THAT SORT OF THING.
WYTHE THEN LEFT THE CONVENTION, NEVER TO RETURN.

WITH ALL THE PRELIMINARIES OVER, IT WAS TIME TO GET DOWN TO BUSINESS.
THE CHAIR RECOGNIZES GOV. RANDOLPH OF VIRGINIA.
HERE GOES.

RANDOLPH MADE A LONG AND FIERY SPEECH DENOUNCING THE ARTICLES OF CONFEDERATION.

HE THEN PRESENTED THE VIRGINIA PLAN.

FORTUNATELY MOST ANTINATIONALISTS HADN'T SHOWN UP YET, OR THERE WOULD HAVE BEEN HELL TO PAY.

THE NEXT PERSON TO TALK WAS CHARLES PINCKNEY, WHO PRESENTED A PLAN OF HIS OWN.*

THERE SHOULD BE A THREE-BRANCHED GOVERNMENT...

IT WAS IGNORED BY EVERYONE, BUT WAS EXTREMELY CLOSE TO THE FINAL CONSTITUTION.

* THE "NEW JERSEY PLAN," WHICH WAS EXACTLY WHAT CONGRESS WANTED (AN IMPROVED ARTICLES OF CONFEDERATION) WOULDN'T BE INTRODUCED FOR ANOTHER MONTH.

OR SO SEZ PINCKNEY

44

CONFLICT!

LATE THE PREVIOUS DAY, THE DELEGATES VOTED TO HAVE THE FIRST BRANCH OF THE LEGISLATURE ELECTED BY THE PEOPLE.

ELECTION OF THE FIRST BRANCH BY THE PEOPLE WAS REAFFIRMED, 7-3.

NEXT CAME THE SECOND BRANCH...

JULY 3rd

WE CANT GO ON LIKE THIS. I MOVE WE APPOINT A GRAND COMMITTEE TO WORK OUT A COMPROMISE.

ONLY PENNSYLVANIA VOTED NO.

WHILE THE REST OF THE CONVENTION TOOK A REST, THE GRAND COMMITTEE WORKED OVER THE JULY 4th HOLIDAY.

ON JULY 5th ELBRIDGE GERRY GAVE THE COMMITTEE REPORT:

1. EACH FIRST BRANCH LEGISLATOR SHALL REPRESENT 40 THOUSAND PEOPLE. HOWEVER, STATES WITH POPULATIONS LESS THAN THAT CAN HAVE ONE ANYWAY.
2. ALL MONEY BILLS SHALL ORIGINATE IN THE FIRST BRANCH. THE SECOND CAN VETO, BUT NOT AMEND THESE BILLS.
3. EQUAL STATE SUFFRAGE IN THE SECOND BRANCH.

(IT WAS ALSO CALLED THE CONNECTICUTT COMPROMISE BECAUSE SHERMAN WAS FROM THERE.

AFTER THAT MORNING THE WHOLE DEMEANOR OF THE CONVENTION CHANGED.
SURE, THERE WERE FIGHTS BUT NOW ALL WERE UNITED IN A SINGLE PURPOSE. THE WORK WENT FAST.

10 DAYS LATER, PHASE TWO WAS OVER. THE VIRGINIA PLAN WAS APPROVED PRETTY MUCH UNCHANGED. A "COMMITTEE OF DETAIL" WAS APPOINTED TO PUT THE NOW 22 RESOLUTIONS IN SOME SORT OF ORDER.

THEN THE CONVENTION WENT ON VACATION FOR TWO WEEKS.

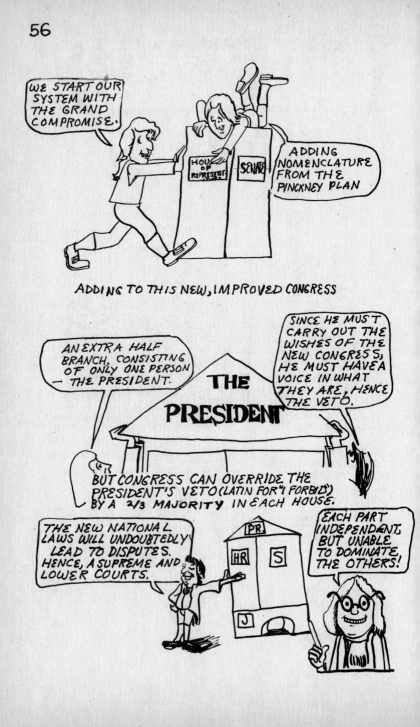

ADDING TO THIS NEW, IMPROVED CONGRESS

BUT AS THE FINAL DRAFT WAS BEING DISCUSSED FOR THE VERY LAST TIME, SOMETHING NEW CAME UP.

I MOVE WE AMEND THE PREAMBLE WITH A DECLARATION OF RIGHTS...

THIS CONSTITUTION IS FINE AS FAR AS IT GOES, BUT AS IT STANDS NOW, FREEDOM CAN BE **OUTLAWED**...

AND IF WE CAN DO **THAT** THE WHOLE THING IS **WORTHLESS!**

BUT, GEORGE, THE WHOLE THING **IS** A DECLARATION OF RIGHTS! WE'VE OUTLAWED BILLS OF ATTAINDER AND EX-POST-FACTO LAWS...

YEAH, BUT IF YOU CAN'T SPEAK YOUR MIND, OR WORSHIP GOD AS YOUR HEART TELLS YOU, OR EVEN GET A FAIR TRIAL, THE REST IS A SICK JOKE!

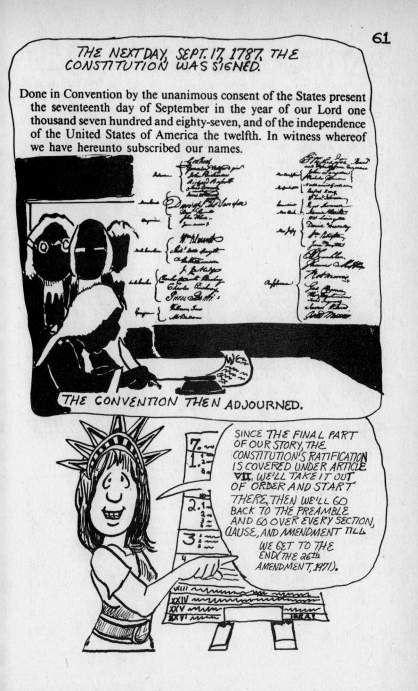

THE NEXT DAY, SEPT. 17, 1787, THE CONSTITUTION WAS SIGNED.

Done in Convention by the unanimous consent of the States present the seventeenth day of September in the year of our Lord one thousand seven hundred and eighty-seven, and of the independence of the United States of America the twelfth. In witness whereof we have hereunto subscribed our names.

THE CONVENTION THEN ADJOURNED.

SINCE THE FINAL PART OF OUR STORY, THE CONSTITUTION'S RATIFICATION IS COVERED UNDER ARTICLE VII, WE'LL TAKE IT OUT OF ORDER AND START THERE, THEN WE'LL GO BACK TO THE PREAMBLE AND GO OVER EVERY SECTION, CLAUSE, AND AMENDMENT TILL WE GET TO THE END (THE 26th AMENDMENT, 1971).

RATIFICATION: ARTICLE VII

The ratification of the conventions of nine States shall be sufficient for the establishment of this Constitution between the States so ratifying the same.

AFTER A VERY SECRET FOUR MONTHS' BEING BORN, THE CONSTITUTION WENT PUBLIC.

AND AS SOON AS IT DID, THE NATION(S) WAS SPLIT INTO TWO GROUPS...

ONE GROUP SUPPORTED THE CONSTITUTION. THEY CALLED THEMSELVES "FEDERALISTS."

THEY WERE LED BY MADISON, HAMILTON, AND GORHAM.

THE OTHER GROUP, WHO DIDN'T, CALLED THEMSELVES REPUBLICANS BUT ARE BETTER KNOWN AS "ANTIFEDERALISTS."

THEY WERE LED BY PATRICK HENRY, GEORGE CLINTON, AND SOMEBODY NAMED WILLIE JONES.

THE FEDERALISTS WERE THE BETTER ORGANIZED OF THE TWO, AND THEY PUSHED IT THROUGH CONGRESS IN LESS THAN A WEEK.

COMIN' THROUGH!

TEN DAYS AFTER THE CONVENTION ENDED, CONGRESS SENT IT TO THE STATES.

EVERYONE, SEMILITERATE DIRT FARMERS INCLUDED, DISCUSSED THE NEW CONSTITUTION.

THE PRESS PUBLISHED ARTICLES BY PEOPLE USING WEIRD PSEUDONYMS LIKE "PUBLIUS" OR "BRUTUS." NOT ALL OF IT WAS ON THE LEVEL OF WHAT WAS LATER CALLED THE "FEDERALIST PAPERS," BUT MOST WAS.

IT WAS AN UNBELIEVABLY WELL-INFORMED ELECTORATE THAT ELECTED DELEGATES TO THE RATIFICATION CONVENTIONS.

THE AVERAGE CONVENTION LASTED A WEEK AND A HALF AND RATIFIED THE CONSTITUTION BY A MARGIN OF TWO TO ONE.

64

RHODE ISLAND REJECTED IT
BY A VOTE OF 2721 to 239.
AND NORTH CAROLINA BY A
SMALLER MARGIN.

MOST CONVENTIONS
DEMANDED A BILL
OF RIGHTS, AND IT
WAS THE PROMISE
OF ONE THAT GOT
VIRGINIA AND NEW
HAMPSHIRE IN.

THREATENED BY THE SECESSION OF THE
CITY, NEW YORK RATIFIED BY TWO VOTES.
IN OCT. 1788, CONGRESS WAS DISSOLVED
AND THE UNITED STATES CEASED TO
EXIST (EXCEPT FOR THE DIPLOMATIC
CORPS AND THE ARMY) UNTIL MARCH 4, 1789.

PART THREE

We
the people
of the United States, in order to form a more
perfect union, establish justice, insure domestic tranquillity,
provide for the common defense, promote the general welfare,
and secure the blessings of liberty to ourselves and our posterity,
do ordain and establish this Constitution for the United States
of America.

ARTICLE I:
CONGRESS

§1: LEGISLATIVE POWER

All legislative powers herein granted shall be vested in a Congress of the United States, which shall consist of a Senate and House of Representatives.

68

THE CONGRESSPERSON WRITES DOWN THE IDEA IN AN ACCEPTABE FORM CALLED A "BILL," WHICH IS FORMALLY INTRODUCED AND SENT TO A SUBCOMMITTEE TO BE RESEARCHED.

THIS CAN BE DONE IN THREE WAYS: THE CONGRESSPERSON CAN: 1. LOOK IT UP IN THE LIBRARY OF CONGRESS.

(THE LIBRARY HAS A COPY OF EVERY BOOK EVER PUBLISHED.* SO SOMETHING IS BOUND TO SHOW UP.)

THEY CAN: 2. GO ON A JUNKET AND SEE THE PROBLEM (IF THERE IS ONE) FOR THEMSELVES.

...I AM PLEASED TO REPORT THAT THE SUNTAN OIL CRISIS IN THE VIRGIN ISLANDS HAS ENDED. IT WAS A DIRTY JOB, BUT, SOMEBODY HAD TO DO IT. YOURS TRULY, ETC. ETC...

THIS IS MORE DANGEROUS THAN IT LOOKS. REP. LEO RYAN WAS KILLED IN GUYANA IN 1978.

*OR SO THE LEGEND GOES.

BUT USUALLY THEY **3.** HOLD A HEARING.

CONGRESSIONAL HEARINGS RANGE FROM SHORT LECTURES ON BORING SUBJECTS TO FULL-BLOWN INVESTIGATIONS LEADING TO PRESIDENTIAL IMPEACHMENTS.

WHISPER WHISPER

MUMBLE

ASIDE FROM BEING AN EXCELLENT RESEARCH TOOL, HEARINGS SERVE AS A WAY OF KEEPING THE EXECUTIVE HONEST, AS WELL AS GENERATING PUBLICITY AND MAKING TROUBLE.

OKAY, A BILL IS THOROUGHLY INVESTIGATED, AND ASSUMING NOBODY GETS HURT, WHERE DO WE GO FROM HERE?

PUTTING IT ALL TOGETHER

OR B) BECOME A LOBBYIST

IT'S EASY TO BECOME A LOBBYIST. ALL YOU HAVE TO DO IS GO TO A CONGRESS PERSON'S OFFICE, WAIT IN HIS LOBBY UNTIL HE/SHE GETS OUT...

ARE THEY GONE YET?

THEN POUNCE

ANOTHER TECHNIQUE USED BY LOBBYISTS IS INDIRECT BRIBERY. IT WORKES LIKE THIS:

LOOK, KIDDO! HAVE YOUR PAC GIVE MY REELECTION COMMITTEE HALF A MILLION BUCKS AND I'LL DEFINITELY VOTE "NO" ON HR 682!

NO SWEAT, JACK.

THE MAIN REASON THAT LOBBYING (BOTH LEGAL AND OTHERWISE) IS SO IMPORTANT IS THAT LOBBYISTS KNOW MUCH MORE ABOUT THEIR SUBJECTS THAN DO THE CONGRESS PEOPLE. IT'S BY FAR THE CHEAPEST WAY THERE IS TO OBTAIN INFORMATION (AND FREE DINNERS).

74

2. No person shall be a representative who shall not have attained to the age of twenty-five years, and been seven years a citizen of the United States, and who shall not, when elected, be an inhabitant of that State in which he shall be chosen.

BUT NOT ALWAYS...

JOHN Y. BROWN (D-KENT.) WAS ELECTED AT THE AGE OF 23, AND TOOK OFFICE AT THE AGE OF 24. (HE WAS LATER EXCLUDED FROM OFFICE BECAUSE HE JOINED THE CONFEDERATE ARMY. A DEFINITE NO-NO IN 1867.)

JOHN Y. BROWN, CSA

THE CENSUS:

3. Representatives and direct taxes shall be apportioned among the several States which may be included within this Union, according to their respective numbers, which shall be determined by adding to the whole number of free persons, including those bound to service for a term of years, and excluding Indians not taxed,

A WORD ABOUT "INDIANS NOT TAXED"

IN THE BEGINNING INDIAN TRIBES WERE TREATED AS THE NATIONS THEY REALLY WERE, FREE AND INDEPENDENT

SO AS FOREIGN NATIONS, THEY WEREN'T TAXED

TREATING ITSELF AS THE EMPIRE IT TRULY WAS, THE USA RESERVED THE RIGHT TO BEAT UP ON ITS NEIGHBORS AND STEAL THEIR LAND.

IT WAS ALL THE RAGE IN THE LATE-NINETEENTH CENTURY.

THE IROQUOIS AND THE SIOUX WENT THE WAY OF THE BASQUES AND ARMENIANS. A TRAGEDY IF THERE EVER WAS ONE.

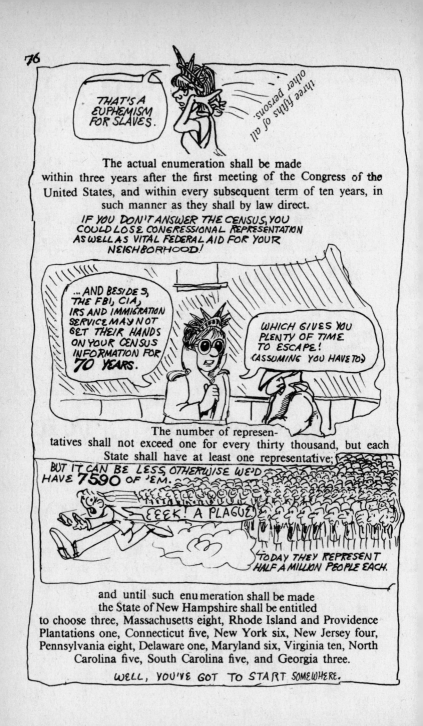

three fifths of all other persons.

THAT'S A EUPHEMISM FOR SLAVES.

The actual enumeration shall be made within three years after the first meeting of the Congress of the United States, and within every subsequent term of ten years, in such manner as they shall by law direct.

IF YOU DON'T ANSWER THE CENSUS, YOU COULD LOSE CONGRESSIONAL REPRESENTATION AS WELL AS VITAL FEDERAL AID FOR YOUR NEIGHBORHOOD!

...AND BESIDES, THE FBI, CIA, IRS AND IMMIGRATION SERVICE MAY NOT GET THEIR HANDS ON YOUR CENSUS INFORMATION FOR 70 YEARS.

WHICH GIVES YOU PLENTY OF TIME TO ESCAPE! (ASSUMING YOU HAVE TO.)

The number of representatives shall not exceed one for every thirty thousand, but each State shall have at least one representative;

BUT IT CAN BE LESS, OTHERWISE WE'D HAVE 7590 OF 'EM.

EEEK! A PLAGUE!

TODAY THEY REPRESENT HALF A MILLION PEOPLE EACH.

and until such enumeration shall be made the State of New Hampshire shall be entitled to choose three, Massachusetts eight, Rhode Island and Providence Plantations one, Connecticut five, New York six, New Jersey four, Pennsylvania eight, Delaware one, Maryland six, Virginia ten, North Carolina five, South Carolina five, and Georgia three.

WELL, YOU'VE GOT TO START SOMEWHERE.

4. When vacancies happen in the representation from any State, the executive authority thereof shall issue writs of election to fill such vacancies.

"TIP" O'NEILL SORT OF PUT IT THIS WAY:

WHEN A SENATE SEAT FALLS VACANT IN THE MIDDLE OF A TERM, THE GOVERNOR OF THE STATE IN QUESTION CAN APPOINT A REPLACEMENT. BUT IF A HOUSE SEAT FALLS VACANT, THERE HAS TO BE A SPECIAL ELECTION.

AND DO YOU KNOW **WHY?** BECAUSE ITS THE **PEOPLE'S HOUSE!!**

QUITE UNLIKE THE OTHER BODY.

5. The House of Representatives shall choose their speaker and other officers;

THE SPEAKER AND HIS MINIONS

THIS (EXCLUDING THE 25th AMENDMENT) IS THE ONLY REFERENCE TO THE SPEAKER IN THE CONSTITUTION, WHICH GIVES HIM A LOT OF LEEWAY ON HOW HE EXERCISES HIS OFFICE.

THE SPEAKER'S MAIN JOB IS TO PRESIDE OVER THE HOUSE...

ORDER! ORDER!

BAM! BAM!

CALL **ME** A WIMP, WILL YOU?!

WHICH MOSTLY MEANS KEEPING ORDER ON THE HOUSE FLOOR.

...and shall have the sole power of impeachment.

IMPEACHMENT

THE IMPEACHMENT PROCESS IS THE ONLY WAY
TO GET RID OF GOVERNMENT OFFICIALS.
IMPEACHMENT IS AN INDICTMENT, AN
ACCUSATION. IT IS ALSO A VERY POTENT
THREAT.

ON JAN. 6, 1932, PROCEEDINGS
BEGAN AGAINST TREASURY
SECRETARY ANDREW MELLON.

LESS THAN 4 MONTHS LATER,
HE HAD RESIGNED AND
HAD FLED THE COUNTRY.

IN MAY OF 1969, A VERY
MINOR SCANDAL INVOLVING
ASSOC. JUSTICE ABE FORTAS
POPPED UP.

IMPEACHMENT

HE WAS GONE IN
TWO WEEKS.

AUGUST 9, 1974: HIS IMPEACHMENT ALL BUT
CERTAIN, RICHARD M. NIXON BECAME THE
FIRST AND ONLY PRESIDENT TO EVER
RESIGN.

♪ I BEG YOUR PARDON.
I NEVER PROMISED YOU
A ROSE GARDEN...

THIS IS WHAT HAPPENS 98% OF THE
TIME. SOMETIMES THE CHARGES, LIKE
THOSE AGAINST PRESIDENT HARRY
TRUMAN OR ASSOC. JUSTICE WILLIAM O.
DOUGLAS, ARE TOTALLY UNFOUNDED.
SO THEY FIGHT BACK, AND WIN.

THEN THERE ARE THOSE LIKE DISTRICT
JUDGE HARRY E. CLAIBORNE, WHO DESPITE
BEING CONVICTED OF A MAJOR FELONY
AND LOSING ALL POSSIBLE APPEALS,
REFUSED TO RESIGN. (THE JOB PAYS
$78 THOUSAND A YEAR.)
THEN AN
IMPEACHMENT
MUST TAKE PLACE.
CLAIBORNE WAS INDEED
IMPEACHED IN LATE
JULY, 1986, 456 to ZERO.
(TO BE CONTINUED.)

JUDGE HARRY

§3: THE SENATE

1. The Senate of the United States shall be composed of two senators from each State, *chosen by the legislature thereof, for six years; and each senator shall have one vote.*

BICAMERALISM* IN A TEACUP:

1790: PRESIDENT WASHINGTON AND SECRETARY OF STATE THOMAS JEFFERSON ARE HANGING OUT AT A LOCAL CAFÉ...

MR. PRESIDENT, HOW COME THE SENATE HAS SUCH A SMALL MEMBERSHIP AND SUCH A LONG TERM?

WHY ARE YOU POURING YOUR TEA IN THAT SAUCER?

TO COOL IT. WHY?

THAT'S WHAT WE DO WITH HOT LEGISLATION FROM THE HOUSE. WE POUR IT INTO THE SENATE...

SOMETIMES IT'S COOLED SO MUCH, THE LEGISLATION FREEZES SOLID.

...TO COOL IT.

ALSO, SENATORS AREN'T ELECTED BY STATE LEGISLATURES ANYMORE. (MORE ON THAT LATER.)

* THE ART OF TWO-HOUSE LEGISLATURES.

2. Immediately after they shall be assembled in consequence of the first election, they shall be divided as equally as may be into three classes. The seats of the senators of the first class shall be vacated at the expiration of the fourth year, and of the third class at the expiration of the sixth year, so that one third may be chosen every second year; and if vacancies happen by resignation, or otherwise, during the recess of the legislature of any State, the executive thereof may make temporary appointments until the next meeting of the legislature, which shall then fill such vacancies.

IT'S IMPERATIVE THAT SOMEBODY KNOWS WHAT'S GOING ON AT ALL TIMES.

3. No person shall be a senator who shall not have attained to the age of thirty years, and been nine years a citizen of the United States, and who shall not, when elected, be an inhabitant of that State for which he shall be chosen.

BUT, THEN AGAIN, HE WAS HENRY CLAY.

THE VICE-PRESIDENCY

4. The Vice President of the United States shall be President of the Senate, but shall have no vote, unless they be equally divided.

THIS WAS PUT HERE IN ORDER TO GIVE THE VICE-PRESIDENT SOMETHING TO DO WHILE WAITING FOR THE PRESIDENT TO GET HIT BY A TRAIN.

SINCE WORLD WAR II VICE-PRESIDENTS HAVE BROKEN ONLY 27 TIES (OUT OF OVER 10 THOUSAND VOTES) WHICH IS WHY THEY ALMOST NEVER PRESIDE.

5. The Senate shall choose their other officers, and also a president *pro tempore,* in the absence of the Vice President, or when he shall exercise the office of the President of the United States.

BEFORE 1890, THE PRESIDENT PRO TEMPORE* WAS ELECTED ANEW EACH TIME THE VEE PEE DIDN'T SHOW UP. ONLY WHEN THE VICE-PRESIDENCY WAS VACANT DID THE JOB HAVE ANY PERMANENCE. SINCE 1890, A PERMANENT PRESIDENT PRO TEMPORE IS ELECTED, AND THE JOB HAS BECOME AN IMITATION SPEAKERSHIP.

IT USUALLY GOES TO THE MOST WRINKLED MEMBER OF THE MAJORITY PARTY. HE USUALLY APPOINTS A JUNIOR MEMBER TO PRESIDE FOR HIM SINCE THE JOB IS SO BORING.

THERE ARE ALSO FLOOR LEADERS AND WHIPS.

*"PRESIDENT FOR NOW" IN LATIN.

IMPEACHMENT, AGAIN

6. The Senate shall have the sole power to try all impeachments. When sitting for that purpose, they shall be on oath or affirmation. When the President of the United States is tried, the chief justice shall preside: and no person shall be convicted without the concurrence of two thirds of the members present.

THE TRIAL OF HARRY CLAIBORNE WAS CONDUCTED LIKE A TYPICAL CONGRESSIONAL INVESTIGATION. FIRST IT WAS SENT TO A SELECT COMMITTEE CREATED FOR THE PURPOSE...

EXCEPT FOR THE FACT THAT IT HAD A DEFENSE ATTORNEY, IT WAS NO DIFFERENT FROM ANY OTHER SENATE INVESTIGATION.

THE COMMITTEE ISSUED A REPORT. AND THEN THE PROCEEDINGS WENT TO THE FLOOR.

IT WAS LIKE ANY OTHER SENATE DEBATE EXCEPT THAT NO SENATORS TOOK PART. THE DEFENSE ATTORNEY AND HOUSE "MANAGERS" (THE PROSECUTORS) DID ALL THE TALKING.

MURDER ISN'T EVEN AN IMPEACHABLE OFFENSE!

OSCAR GOODMAN, CLAIBORNE'S LAWYER, WHILE TRYING TO GET A RESTRAINING ORDER, GOT CHIEF JUSTICE WILLIAM REHNQUIST TO MAKE THE DEFINITIVE PRONOUNCEMENT ON THE SUBJECT.

THE JUDICIARY HAS NOTHING TO DO WITH IMPEACHMENT.

CLAIBORNE WAS REMOVED FROM OFFICE.

7. Judgment in cases of impeachment shall not extend further than to removal from office, and disqualifications to hold and enjoy any office of honor, trust or profit under the United States: but the party convicted shall nevertheless be liable and subject to indictment, trial, judgment and punishment, according to law.

THE REASON WHY ONLY ONE PERSON HAS BEEN IMPEACHED IN FIFTY YEARS IS THAT "RETIRED JUDGE" AND "FORMER PRESIDENT" ARE OFFICES OF "TRUST AND PROFIT." IF YOU'RE CONVICTED, BYE-BYE, PENSION!

...AND ANOTHER THING, THE REFERENCE TO THE CHIEF JUSTICE IS THE ONLY ONE IN THE ENTIRE CONSTITUTION.

...WHICH MEANS THAT WHILE THERE HAS TO BE ONE, THE TITLE IS ALMOST PURELY HONORARY. HE IS ON THE SUPREME COURT BY VIRTUE OF THE JUDICIARY ACT OF 1789, NOT THE CONSTITUTION.

§4: LAME DUCKS
& OTHERS

1. The times, places, and manner of holding elections for senators and representatives, shall be prescribed in each State by the legislature thereof; but the Congress may at any time by law make or alter such regulations, except as to the places of choosing senators.

THIS WAS PUT HERE SO THE STATES WOULDN'T AUTHORIZE RIGGED ELECTIONS. IT ALSO PERMITS CONGRESS TO ESTABLISH A UNIFORM ELECTION DAY THROUGHOUT THE NATION.

2. The Congress shall assemble at least once in every year, and such meeting shall be on the ⅔ unless they shall by law appoint a different day.

THIS BIT WAS REPEALED IN 1933.

THE REASON WAS AN INTENTIONAL MISTAKE AT THE VERY BEGINNING.

rst Monday in Decemb

INSTEAD OF STARTING THE NEW GOVERNMENT IN DECEMBER 1788 LIKE IT SHOULD HAVE, THE OLD CONGRESS SET THE STARTING DATE THREE MONTHS LATER, ON MARCH 4, 1789.

RIGHT WAY

WRONG WAY

THOUGH IT MAY HAVE SEEMED LIKE A GOOD IDEA AT THE TIME, IT COMPLETELY SCREWED UP THE RHYTHM THE FRAMERS HAD TRIED TO SET UP...

INSTEAD OF TWO SESSIONS OF EQUAL LENGTH PER CONGRESS, THERE WERE NOW LONG AND SHORT SESSIONS.

THE LONG SESSIONS WENT ALONG LIKE THEY WERE SUPPOSED TO...

THE SHORT SESSIONS, WITH NINE MONTHS' WORK TO DO IN THREE MONTHS' TIME, WERE TOTAL CHAOS.

AND THINGS GOT WORSE IN 1872, WHEN A STANDARDIZED ELECTION DAY WAS ESTABLISHED...

ELECTION DAY WAS (AND IS) THE FIRST TUESDAY AFTER THE FIRST MONDAY IN NOVEMBER IN EVEN-NUMBERED YEARS. UNFORTUNATELY, THE **PREVIOUS** CONGRESS BEGAN A MONTH LATER...

WHICH MEANT THAT MANY PEOPLE WHO HAD **LOST** WENT TO WASHINGTON INSTEAD OF THE WINNERS.

AND SO, WITH NO SEMBLANCE OF A MANDATE AT ALL, THEY "HOBBLED AROUND LIKE LAME DUCKS."

HENCE THE NAME.

AND NOT ONLY THAT, A CONGRESSPERSON-ELECT HAD TO WAIT OVER A YEAR TO TAKE HIS SEAT.

LIKE I SAID, IT'S BEEN REPEALED.*

*THE 20th AMENDMENT, P. 210

§5: RULES, REGS, CENSURES & EXPULSIONS

1. Each House shall be the judge of the elections, returns

THIS LETS CONGRESS FIGURE OUT WHO WON IN CASE OF A TIE.

FR'INSTANCE IN 1984... FRANK McCLOSKEY BEAT RICHARD McINTYRE BY 4 (THAT'S FOUR) VOTES OUT OF 200 THOUSAND.

OR DID HE?

WE'LL PROBABLY NEVER KNOW. BUT AFTER FIVE MONTHS OF WRANGLING, THAT'S WHAT A SELECT COMMITTEE FINALLY DECIDED.

SO WE'LL HAVE TO TAKE THEIR WORD FOR IT.

REMEMBER, EVERY VOTE COUNTS!

TIES, LIKE THE 1974 NEW HAMPSHIRE SENATE RACE, CAN HAPPEN AT ANY TIME, ESPECIALLY IF NO ONE VOTES.

...and qualifications of its own members,

THIS LETS CONGRESS REFUSE TO SEAT ANY 16-YEAR-OLD ILLEGAL ALIEN WHO MIGHT GET ELECTED. (LORD KNOWS HOW.)

BUT WHAT ABOUT OTHER REASONS? LIKE BEING A CROOK, FOR INSTANCE...

THE ANSWER IS NO, OF COURSE. BUT THAT DOESN'T MEAN THAT IT HASN'T BEEN TRIED, HOWEVER.

THE CASE:

POWELL v. McCORMACK

(1969, 395 U.S. 486)

QUESTION:
CAN THE HOUSE (OR THE SENATE) EXCLUDE ANYBODY FOR ANY REASON?

REP. ADAM C. POWELL JR.

SPEAKER JOHN McCORMACK

A LOT OF PEOPLE HAD IT IN FOR ADAM POWELL...

THE FIERY HARLEM PREACHER-CUM-CONGRESSMAN HAD BEEN AT THE FOREFRONT OF THE CIVIL RIGHTS MOVEMENT OF THE 1940's, '50's AND '60's. HE HAD ALMOST SINGLE-HANDEDLY DESEGREGATED THE CAPITOL IN 1943...

SELMA, MONTGOMERY, THE MARCH ON WASHINGTON, HE WAS THERE. HIS "POWELL AMENDMENTS" HELPED END SEGREGATION IN THE FEDERAL GOVERNMENT.

FREEDOM NOW!

ADAM POWELL WAS A HERO!

HE WAS WITTY AND AUDACIOUS AND HIS CONSTITUENTS LOVED HIM FOR IT. BUT RACISM WASN'T COMPLETELY OUT OF FASHION IN 1967.

AND THOSE RACISTS CHORTLED WITH GLEE WHEN HE GOT CAUGHT EMBEZZLING OVER $40 THOUSAND.

HEE HEE HEE

ALABAM POWELL IN

ON JANUARY 10, 1967, POWELL WAS ASKED TO STEP ASIDE DURING THE TRADITIONAL OATH-TAKING, ON THE GROUNDS THAT HE WAS UNQUALIFIED.

A SELECT COMMITTEE, CHAIRED BY REP. EMANUEL CELLER, WAS APPOINTED TO INVESTIGATE THE CHARGE.

MAY WE SEE YOUR DRIVER'S LICENSE, MR. POWELL?

IT FOUND THAT ALTHOUGH POWELL WAS INDEED A CROOK, HE WAS MORE THAN QUALIFIED TO TAKE HIS SEAT...

...HOWEVER, HE SHOULD BE CENSURED AND MADE TO PAY BACK WHAT HE STOLE.

THE HOUSE AS A WHOLE, HOWEVER, DIDN'T AGREE AND POWELL WAS EXCLUDED BY A VOTE OF 222-202.

NOW A MARTYR, HE **EASILY** WON A SPECIAL ELECTION A MONTH LATER. HE ALSO SUED SPEAKER JOHN McCORMACK AND MOST OTHER HOUSE OFFICERS.

POWELL CHOSE NOT TO TAKE HIS SEAT WHILE HIS CASE WAFTED ITS WAY THROUGH THE COURTS. INSTEAD, HE WENT INTO SELF-IMPOSED EXILE AT HIS LUSH VILLA IN THE BAHAMAS.

HE WAS REELECTED AGAIN IN 1968. THIS TIME HE WAS SEATED. (MAINLY BECAUSE HE PAID BACK HIS ILL-GOTTEN GAINS.) THE CASE GOT TO THE SUPREME COURT IN 1969.

CHIEF JUSTICE EARL WARREN READ THE OPINION:

THE HOUSE'S EXCLUSION OF MR. POWELL WAS UNCONSTITUTIONAL! EXTRA QUALIFICATIONS MAY NOT BE ADDED TO THE ONES ALREADY ENUMERATED.

IN OTHER WORDS, YOU CAN'T FIGHT CRIME WITH CRIME.

and a majority of
each shall constitute a quorum to do business; but a smaller number
may adjourn from day to day, and may be authorized to compel
the attendance of absent members, in such manner, and under such
penalties as each House may provide.

QUORUMS ARE CALLED SEVERAL TIMES
A DAY. AS FAR AS WE CAN TELL, NOBODY
HAS EVER BEEN PUNISHED FOR PLAYING HOOKY.

2. Each House may determine the rules of its proceedings,

AS WE'VE SEEN, EACH HOUSE IS QUITE DIFFERENT FROM ITS COUNTERPART.

AND THE DIFFERENCES BECOME QUITE APPARENT ONCE A BILL COMES OUT OF COMMITTEE.

THE HOUSE **THE SENATE**

ONCE A BILL PASSES A COMMITTEE, IT HAS TO WAIT IN LINE BEFORE GETTING OUT ON THE FLOOR.

ONCE A BILL PASSES A COMMITTEE, IT HAS TO WAIT IN LINE BEFORE GETTING OUT ON THE FLOOR.

THERE ARE FIVE LINES, ACTUALLY, WHICH ARE CALLED "CALENDARS."

THERE ARE TWO LINES, ACTUALLY, WHICH ARE CALLED "CALENDARS."

1. THE UNION CALENDAR:
THIS IS WHERE LEGISLATION RAISING OR COSTING MONEY GOES. THESE ARE FIRST DEBATED IN THE "COMMITTEE OF THE WHOLE ON THE STATE OF THE UNION."

2. THE HOUSE CALENDAR:
BILLS THAT DON'T COST ANYTHING BUT ARE IMPORTANT ANYWAY GO HERE.

1. THE LEGISLATIVE CALENDAR:
WHICH IS WHERE ALL LEGISLATION GOES.

2. THE EXECUTIVE CALENDAR
WHICH IS WHERE EXECUTIVE AND JUDICIARY NOMINATIONS, AS WELL AS TREATIES, GO.

HERE IT IS SUPPOSED TO WAIT ONE LEGISLATIVE DAY.

3. THE CONSENT CALENDAR:

NON-CONTROVERSIAL BILLS LIKE "NATIONAL BANANA PEEL DAY" CAN GO HERE.

4. THE PRIVATE CALENDAR:

THIS IS FOR BILLS THAT HELP INDIVIDUAL PEOPLE GET PENSIONS OR KEEP FROM GETTING DEPORTED.

5. THE DISCHARGE CALENDAR

BILLS HAVING TO DO WITH THE LOCAL AFFAIRS IN THE DISTRICT OF COLUMBIA AND DISCHARGE PETITIONS THAT TRY TO GET BILLS OUT OF COMMITTEE GET PUT HERE.

BUT GETTING ON A CALENDAR DOESN'T MEAN THAT YOU CAN GET ON THE FLOOR...

FIRST YOU NEED A TICKET, CALLED A RULE. THEY ARE AVAILABLE AT THE TICKET OFFICE...

ONE, PLEASE.

...CALLED THE "RULES COMMITTEE"

AS YOU MAY HAVE GUESSED, THE RULES COMMITTEE IS VERY POWERFUL.

RULES CONTROL DEBATE ON THE FLOOR. THE RULES COMMITTEE CAN ASSIGN IT ONE OF SEVERAL TYPES BEFORE LETTING IT ON THE FLOOR.

HAVE I GOT A RULE FOR YOU!

BUT THERE IS SOMETHING STRANGE ABOUT THE "LEGISLATIVE DAY"

MON 3 MON 3 MON
MON 3 MON 3 M
MON MON

A LEGISLATIVE DAY IS THE TIME FROM CONVENING TO ADJOURNING FOR THE NIGHT, WHICH THE SENATE DOESN'T ALWAYS DO. SOMETIMES IT RECESSES FOR THE NIGHT INSTEAD.

WHICH MEANS THAT IT DOESN'T HAVE TO START OVER FROM SCRATCH, BUT IT REMAINS THE SAME "DAY" AS THE ONE BEFORE. A "DAY" CAN LAST SIX MONTHS.

BUT THIS RULE CAN BE SUSPENDED; IT ALMOST ALWAYS IS.

ONCE A BILL GETS ON A CALENDAR, THE CHAIRMAN OF THE BILL'S COMMITTEE GOES TO THE OFFICE OF THE SENATE MAJORITY LEADER...

KNOCK! KNOCK! KNOCK!

THE TWO SENATORS THEN GO TO THE OFFICE OF THE MINORITY LEADER TO NEGOTIATE WHAT IS CALLED A "UNANIMOUS CONSENT AGREEMENT."

92

punish its members for disorderly behavior,

ON FEB. 22, 1902, SENATORS BENJAMIN TILLMAN
AND JOHN McLAURIN (BOTH D-S.C.) GOT INTO
A MAJOR FISTFIGHT OVER THE U.S. CONQUEST
OF THE PHILIPPINES.

THIS IS KNOWN AS
DISORDERLY BEHAVIOR.
BOTH WERE CENSURED.

SINCE THEN, HOWEVER, CENSURE HAS BEEN
USED MAINLY FOR CORRUPTION, A PRACTICE
THAT IS USUALLY FROWNED UPON.

THERE WAS,
HOWEVER, ONE
PERSON WHO
WAS CENSURED
FOR A VERY
DIFFERENT
REASON. HIS
NAME WAS
JOE McCARTHY.

IN A FOUR-YEAR-
LONG REIGN OF
TERROR, McCARTHY
RUINED MORE LIVES
IN PEACETIME THAN
ANYONE ELSE IN
CONGRESSIONAL
HISTORY (OR AT LEAST
SINCE 1920).
IN 1954, A DISGUSTED
SENATE CONDEMNED
HIM. OFFICIALLY IT
WAS FOR NOT COOPERATING
WITH THE SENATE
CENSURE COMMITTEE
(WHICH WAS TRUE),
BUT REALLY FOR
ATTEMPTING TO DESTROY
AMERICAN FREEDOM
(AND ALMOST SUCCEEDING.)

and with the concurrence of
two thirds, expel a member.

SINCE THE CIVIL WAR, ONLY ONE PERSON
HAS BEEN ACTUALLY EXPELLED.
REP. OZZIE MYERS GOT CAUGHT
IN THE ABSCAM NET IN 1979.

3. Each House shall keep a journal of its proceedings, and from time to time publish the same, excepting such parts as may in their judgment require secrecy; and the yeas and nays of the members of either House on any question shall, at the desire of one fifth of those present, be entered on the journal.

IT'S CALLED THE CONGRESSIONAL RECORD. IT IS PUBLISHED DAILY AND ITS FULL OF SPEECHES THAT WERE NEVER GIVEN. USUALLY IT'S LOTS OF FUN TO READ. YOU CAN GET IT AT THE PUBLIC LIBRARY (SOMETIMES).

4. Neither House, during the session of Congress, shall, without the consent of the other, adjourn for more than three days, nor to any other place than that in which the two Houses shall be sitting.

WHICH MEANS THAT WITHOUT THE HOUSE'S PERMISSION, THE SENATE MAY NOT GO TO LAS VEGAS FOR THE WEEKEND.

§6: PRIVILEGES & IMMUNITIES (OF CONGRESSPEOPLE)

1. The senators and representatives shall receive a compensation for their services, to be ascertained by law, and paid out of the Treasury of the United States.

YOU EXPECT US TO DO THIS FOR FREE?

They shall in all cases, except treason, felony, and breach of the peace, be privileged from arrest during their attendance at the session of their respective Houses, and in going to and returning from the same; and for any speech or debate in either House, they shall not be questioned in any other place.

REP. ADAM CLAYTON POWELL SAID SOME NASTY THINGS ABOUT MRS. ESTHER JAMES ON THE FLOOR OF THE HOUSE.

THESE REMARKS WERE LIBELOUS. BUT SHE COULDN'T DO ANYTHING ABOUT IT BECAUSE POWELL WAS IMMUNE — HOWEVER... WHEN HE REPEATED THE CHARGE ON MEET THE PRESS, SHE WAS FREE TO SUE, WHICH SHE DID. SHE GOT A HEFTY JUDGMENT

2. No senator or representative shall, during the time for which he was elected, be appointed to any civil office under the authority of the United States, which shall have been created, or the emoluments whereof shall have been increased during such time; and no person holding any office under the United States shall be a member of either House during his continuance in office.

IT WAS FEARED THAT THE EXECUTIVE BRANCH WOULD ATTEMPT TO DOMINATE THE LEGISLATIVE BRANCH.

...AND THEY HAVE...

...BUT THEY CAN'T...

SO THERE!

§7: THE VETO

1. All bills for raising revenue shall originate in the House of Representatives; but the Senate may propose or concur with amendments as on other bills.

IT DOESN'T ALWAYS HAPPEN THAT WAY. SOMETIMES THE HOUSE PREFERS THAT IT DOESN'T.

EEEK!

IF THE HOUSE DOESN'T LIKE A MONEY BILL ORIGINATING IN THE SENATE, IT CAN ISSUE A "BLUE SLIP"

...WHICH KILLS IT.

2. Every bill which shall have passed the House of Representatives and the Senate, shall, before it becomes a law, be presented to the President of the United States;

H.R. 1742!

HI, THERE, LITTLE GUY!

if he approves he shall sign it, but...

HOW DO YOU SPELL "R"?

...if not he shall return it, with his objections to that House in which it shall have originated, who shall enter the objections at large on their journal, and proceed to reconsider it.

WAAAA!

VETO

POOR BABY!

YIPPEE!

GRUMBLE MUMBLE

If after such reconsideration two thirds of that House shall agree to pass the bill, it shall be sent, together with the objections, to the other House, by which it shall likewise be reconsidered, and if approved by two thirds of that House, it shall become a law.

But in all such cases the votes of both Houses shall be determined by yeas and nays, and the names of the persons voting for and against the bill shall be entered on the journal of each House respectively.

THE ALL-TIME VETO CHAMPION WAS GROVER CLEVELAND, WHO VETOED 413(!) BILLS IN ONLY FOUR YEARS!

HEE! HEE! HEE!

If any bill shall not be returned by the President within ten days (Sundays excepted) after it shall have been presented to him, the same shall be a law, in like manner as if he had signed it,

unless the Congress by their adjournment prevent its return, in which case it shall not be a law.

LEGEND HAS IT THAT AFTER CONGRESS ADJOURNS, THE PRESIDENT PUTS BILLS IN HIS POCKET AND FORGETS ABOUT THEM.

HENCE, THIS METHOD'S CALLED A "POCKET VETO"

LET ME OUTTA HERE!

3. Every order, resolution, or vote to which the concurrence of the Senate and the House of Representatives may be necessary (except on a question of adjournment) shall be presented to the President of the United States; and before the same shall take effect, shall be approved by him, or being disapproved by him, shall be repassed by two thirds of the Senate and House of Representatives, according to the rules and limitations prescribed in the case of a bill.

§8: WHAT CONGRESS CAN DO

The Congress shall have the power

NOW THAT WE HAVE A LEGISLATIVE SYSTEM SET UP, WHAT GOOD IS IT IF IT CAN'T DO ANYTHING, RIGHT? (HANG ON, FOLKS, THIS IS THE LONGEST SECTION OF THE ENTIRE CONSTITUTION)

1. To lay and collect taxes, duties, imposts, and excises, to pay the debts and provide for the common defense and general welfare of the United States; but all duties, imposts, and excises shall be uniform throughout the United States;

2. To borrow money on the credit of the United States;

3. To regulate commerce with foreign nations, and among the several States, and with the Indian tribes;

FR'INSTANCE...

IN THE 1810'S NEW YORK PASSED A LAW FORCING STEAMBOAT OWNERS TO BUY A PRIVATELY ISSUED LICENSE, UNDER PAIN OF LOSING ONE'S BOAT.

NEW JERSEY AND CONNECTICUT, WHO SHARED WATERWAYS WITH NEW YORK AND ALSO LICENSED STEAMBOATS, DIDN'T LIKE THIS AT ALL.

...ESPECIALLY SINCE THEY WERE LOSING THEIR BOATS.

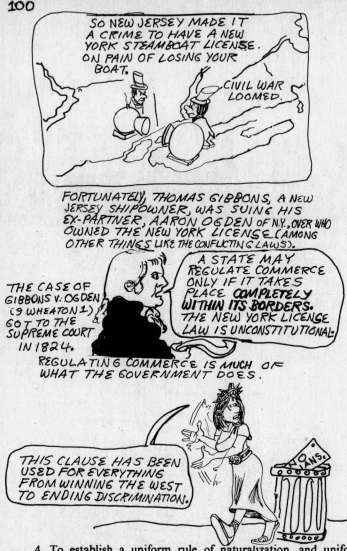

4. To establish a uniform rule of naturalization, and uniform laws on the subject of bankruptcies throughout the United States;

5. To coin money, regulate the value thereof, and of foreign coin, and fix the standard of weights and measures;

6. To provide for the punishment of counterfeiting the securities and current coin of the United States;

7. To establish post offices and post roads;

8. To promote the progress of science and useful arts, by securing for limited times to authors and inventors the exclusive right to their respective writings and discoveries;

9. To constitute tribunals inferior to the Supreme Court;
SEE ARTICLE III, PAGES 126 -135.

10. To define and punish piracies and felonies committed on the high seas, and offenses against the law of nations;

11. To declare war, grant letters of marque and reprisal, and make rules concerning captures on land and water;

12. To raise and support armies, but no appropriation of money to that use shall be for a longer term than two years;

13. To provide and maintain a navy;

14. To make rules for the government and regulation of the land and naval forces;

15. To provide for calling forth the militia to execute the laws of the Union, suppress insurrections and repel invasions;

16. To provide for organizing, arming, and disciplining the militia, and for governing such part of them as may be employed in the service of the United States, reserving to the States respectively, the appointment of the officers, and the authority of training the militia according to the discipline prescribed by Congress.

A LETTER OF MARQUE AND REPRISAL IS A
PIRATE'S LICENSE. THEY DON'T ISSUE
THEM ANYMORE

MILITARY APPROPRIATIONS
ARE GOOD ONLY FOR TWO
YEARS.

THIS KEEPS THE GENERALS
HUMBLE.

PLEASE
GIVE ME A
HUNDRED BILLION
DOLLARS. I'LL
BE YOUR BEST
FRIEND!

NO!

17. To exercise legislation in all cases whatsoever, over such
district (not exceeding ten miles square) as may, by cession of
particular States, and the acceptance of Congress, become the seat
of the government of the United States, and to exercise like authority
over all places purchased by the consent of the legislature of the
State in which the same shall be, for the erection of forts, magazines,
arsenals, dockyards, and other needful buildings; and ...

D.C.,

THE DISTRICT OF COLUMBIA WAS CREATED
FOR ONE PURPOSE: TO AVOID HAVING THE
FEDERAL GOVERNMENT KICKED OUT OF
WHERE IT WAS CURRENTLY HANGING OUT
BY THE STATE OR LOCALITY HAVING
JURISDICTION.

AND STAY
OUT!

THE CITY OF WASHINGTON WAS FOUNDED IN 1800. CONGRESS GAVE IT A DEMOCRATIC GOVERNMENT SIMILAR TO EVERY OTHER CITY IN THE COUNTRY AT THE TIME.

UNTIL JUST AFTER THE CIVIL WAR, WASHINGTON WAS JUST ANOTHER SLEEPY SOUTHERN TOWN. (EXCEPT FOR 1814 WHEN THE BRITISH BURNT IT TO THE GROUND.)

THEN IN 1865 EVERYTHING CHANGED.

SLAVERY WAS ENDED AND NATIVE-BORN PEOPLE OF AFRICAN DESCENT BECAME AMERICAN CITIZENS.

THOUSANDS OF "FREEDMEN," AS THEY WERE CALLED, MOVED TO WASHINGTON.

BY 1870, THEY HAD BECOME A SUBSTANTIAL PART OF THE POPULATION, AND A MAJOR FORCE IN LOCAL POLITICS.

HELLO THERE, FRIEND, I'M RUNNING FOR CITY COUNCIL.

EEEK! A NIGGAH!

UNFORTUNATELY, RACISTS WERE ALSO A SUBSTANTIAL PART OF THE POPULATION.

18. To make all laws which shall be necessary and proper for carrying into execution the foregoing powers, and all other powers vested by this Constitution in the government of the United States, or in any department or officer thereof.

THERE WERE TWO BASIC ISSUES IN THE CASE:

1. COULD THE FEDERAL GOVERNMENT SET UP A BANK?

YES! SOME BANKING FUNCTIONS ARE NEEDED TO MAKE THE GOVERNMENT RUN PROPERLY!

NO! NOWHERE DOES IT SAY THAT THE GOVERNMENT CAN DO THAT!

2. CAN A STATE TAX THE FEDERAL GOVERNMENT?

SEE PAGE 149 FOR THE EXCITING ANSWER!

CHIEF JUSTICE JOHN MARSHALL'S OPINION WENT LIKE THIS...

ART. I §8 CL. 18 WAS PUT THERE TO MAKE CONGRESS'S JOB EASIER, AND A BANK CERTAINLY DOES THAT. SO IT'S LEGAL.

AS FAR AS TAXING IT GOES, ART. VI §2 STATES THAT ALL FEDERAL TO BE CONTINUED

§9: WHAT CONGRESS CAN'T DO

THIS WAS WHAT WAS SUPPOSED TO BE THE BILL OF RIGHTS.

AS YOU CAN SEE, IT WAS PAINFULLY INADEQUATE.

1. The migration or importation of such persons as any of the States now existing shall think proper to admit, shall not be prohibited by the Congress prior to the year one thousand eight hundred and eight, but a tax or duty may be imposed on such importation, not exceeding ten dollars for each person.

THE WORST CLAUSE IN THE CONSTITUTION, IT CONDEMNED MILLIONS OF INNOCENT PEOPLE TO MISERY AND DEATH. THE $10 MAXIMUM DUTY WAS MEANT TO MAKE THIS HORRIBLE PRACTICE EASIER. BE GRATEFUL IT IS NOW DEFUNCT.

2. The privilege of the writ of *habeas corpus* shall not be suspended, unless when in cases of rebellion or invasion the public safety may require it.

THE WRIT OF HABEAS CORPUS (LATIN FOR "HAVE A BODY") IS AN ORDER BY A JUDGE TO A POLICE AUTHORITY TO BRING A PERSON UNDER ARREST

WHY DID YOU ARREST THIS MAN?

BECAUSE HE LOOKS LIKE MY EX-WIFE, YOUR HONOR.

TO THE JUDGE'S CHAMBERS AND EXPLAIN WHY THE POOR SUCKER GOT BUSTED. IF THE COP DOESN'T HAVE A GOOD REASON, THE ARRESTEE IS FREED.

WHEN HABEAS CORPUS IS SUSPENDED, SO ARE ALL RIGHTS. A PERSON CAN BE HELD WITHOUT CHARGE INDEFINITELY. THIS CAN ONLY BE DONE, HOWEVER, DURING A CIVIL WAR OR INVASION.

LET ME OUT OF HERE!

THE LAST TIME HABEAS CORPUS WAS SUSPENDED IN THE "LOWER 48" WAS IN SOUTH CAROLINA IN 1872. IT WAS SUSPENDED BY THE GOVERNOR OF HAWAII IN 1941, BUT THE SUPREME COURT HELD THAT ACTION UNCONSTITUTIONAL (DUNCAN V. Kahanamuku (372 U.S. 304, 1946).

4. No capitation, or other direct, tax shall be laid, unless in proportion to the census or enumeration hereinbefore directed to be taken.

IN 200 YEARS NOBODY'S FIGURED OUT HOW TO DO IT.

WHICH IS WHY THEY PASSED THE 16th AMENDMENT.

5. No tax or duty shall be laid on articles exported from any State.

6. No preference shall be given by any regulation of commerce or revenue to the ports of one State over those of another: nor shall vessels bond to, or from, one State be obliged to enter, clear, or pay duties in another.

AS BEN FRANKLIN SO APTLY PUT IT,

THE POWER TO TAX IS THE POWER TO DESTROY!

SO STATES ARE PROTECTED FROM BEING BEATEN UP BY THE FEDS.

7. No money shall be drawn from the treasury, but in consequence of appropriations made by law; and a regular statement and account of the receipts and expenditures of all public money shall be published from time to time.

SWIPING GOVERNMENT MOOLAH IS A NO-NO.

8. No title of nobility shall be granted by the United States: and no person holding any office or profit or trust under them, shall, without the consent of the Congress, accept of any present, emolument, office, or title, of any kind whatever, from any king, prince, or foreign State.

IN OTHER WORDS, NO BRIBE TAKING.

MEDALS FROM ALLIES IN WARTIME ARE OKAY, HOWEVER.

$1 EXPLANATIONS, WHYS, HOWS, WHERE-FORS & A FEW HOO-HA'S

1. The executive power shall be vested in a President of the United States of America.

WE CAN ASK THE SAME QUESTIONS ABOUT EXECUTIVE POWER AS WE DID ABOUT LEGISLATIVE.

1. WHAT IS EXECUTIVE POWER?

EXECUTIVE POWER IS THE ABILITY TO TAKE CONGRESS'S MANDATES AND PUT 'EM INTO ACTION!

CONGRESS GIVES THE ORDERS, AND THE PRESIDENT (OR ONE OF HIS MILLIONS OF SUBORDINATES) CARRIES IT OUT.

2. HOW DOES IT WORK?

LET'S SAY THAT CONGRESS VOTES A NATIONAL HIGHWAY PROJECT...

THE SECRETARY OF TRANSPORTATION GIVES ABOUT $20 MILLION OR SO TO AN ASSISTANT UNDER-SECRETARY, WHO GRABS SOME ENGINEERS, SOME WORK CREWS AND LOTS OF EQUIPMENT. THEY THEN GO OUT AND BUILD IT. SED UNTIL 2031

...THUS TYING UP TRAFFIC FOR YEARS.

EXECUTIVE POWER RUNS THE GAMBIT FROM WRITING BOOKS ON GROWING BETTER RUTABAGAS TO BLOWING UP THE WORLD.

OFFICIALLY, ALL EXECUTIVE POWER BELONGS TO THE PRESIDENT AND NOBODY ELSE.

SO AN ASSISTANT UNDERSECRETARY IS ONLY AN ARM OF THE SINGLE PRESIDENT, WHO CAN FIRE HIM/HER AT ANY MOMENT.

OR TRY TO. IN 1868 PRES. ANDREW JOHNSON WAS IMPEACHED FOR DOING JUST THAT.

IN 1867, PRESIDENT JOHNSON VIOLATED THE UNCONSTITUTIONAL TENURE OF OFFICE ACT.

AFTER A UNIQUE, EXCITING, AND VERY NASTY TRIAL, JOHNSON WAS ACQUITTED BY ONE VOTE. THIS SAVED THE PRESIDENCY AND MAYBE EVEN THE NATION.

TODAY, THE PRESIDENT CAN FIRE ANY MEMBER OF THE EXECUTIVE BRANCH.

3. HOW DO I GET SOME?

ASIDE FROM GETTING ELECTED PRESIDENT YOURSELF (A VERRRY IFFY SITUATION EVEN IN THE BEST OF CIRCUMSTANCES) THERE ARE TWO BASIC METHODS:

1. TAKE THE CIVIL SERVICE EXAM.

FOR THE LOW TO MIDDLE LEVEL POSITIONS, THIS IS THE ONLY WAY TO DO IT, AND IT ISN'T THAT HARD...

2. HELP SOMEBODY ELSE GET ELECTED PRESIDENT.

IF YOU'RE A HARD WORKER, AND YOU GET ON A WINNING CAMPAIGN, THERE'S A FAIR CHANCE YOU'LL GET AN UPPER-MIDDLE LEVEL POSITION.

He shall hold his office during
the term of four years, and, together with the Vice President, chosen
for the same term, be elected as follows:

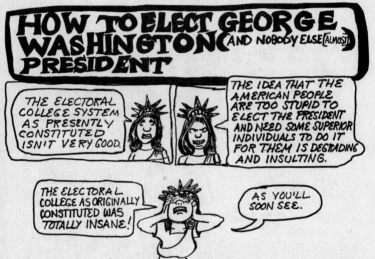

2. Each State shall appoint, in such manner as the legislature
thereof may direct, a number of electors, equal to the whole number
of senators and representatives to which the State may be entitled
in the congress: but no senator or representative, or person holding
an office of trust or profit under the United States, shall be appointed
an elector.

*THIS LAST SENTENCE WAS PUT HERE SO THAT
NOBODY COULD VOTE FOR PRESIDENT TWICE.
THE FRAMERS THOUGHT THE PRESIDENTIAL
ELECTION WOULD GET THROWN INTO THE HOUSE
EVERY TIME.*

The electors shall meet in their respective States, and vote by
ballot for two persons, of whom one at least shall not be an
inhabitant of the same State with themselves. And they shall make
a list of all the persons voted for, and of the number of votes for
each; which list they shall sign and certify, and transmit sealed to
the seat of the government of the United States, directed to the
president of the Senate. The president of the Senate shall, in the
presence of the Senate and House of Representatives, open all the
certificates, and the votes shall then be counted. The person having
the greatest number of votes shall be the President, if such number
be a majority of the whole number of electors appointed; and if
there be more than one who have such majority, and have an equal
number of votes, then the House of Representatives shall immediately

choose by ballot one of them for President; and if no person have a majority, then from the five highest on the list the said House shall in like manner choose the President. But in choosing the President, the votes shall be taken by States, the representation from each State having one vote; a quorum for this purpose shall consist of a member or members from two thirds of the States, and a majority of all the States shall be necessary to a choice. In every case, after the choice of the President, the person having the greatest number of votes of the electors shall be the Vice President. But if there should remain two or more who have equal votes, the Senate shall choose from them by ballot the Vice President.

THIS ONLY WORKED IN THE FIRST TWO ELECTIONS BECAUSE GEORGE WASHINGTON WAS ELECTED UNANIMOUSLY BOTH TIMES.

OOO! THE SUSPENSE!

...AND THE ELECTORS VOTED FOR THEIR SECOND FAVORITE CANDIDATE, WHO BECAME VEEPEE.

IN THE THIRD ELECTION (1796) THE PRESIDENT (JOHN ADAMS) WAS OF ONE PARTY, WHILE THE VICE-PRESIDENT (THOMAS JEFFERSON) WAS OF ANOTHER. THE BICKERING ALMOST STARTED A CIVIL WAR. BOTH SIDES VOWED THAT IN 1800 THEY WOULD GET IT RIGHT.

THE TIE TO END ALL TIES

WHILE THE CAMPAIGN OF 1800 WASN'T THE NASTIEST IN HISTORY, IT WAS UP THERE.

IN THE END, VICE-PRESIDENT JEFFERSON AND HIS RUNNING MATE AARON BURR, BEAT PRESIDENT ADAMS AND C.C. PINCKNEY BY A MODERATE AMOUNT. JEFFERSON WAS ELECTED...

3. The Congress may determine the time of choosing the electors, and the day on which they shall give their votes; which day shall be the same throughout the United States.

WHY NOT?

4. No person except a natural born citizen, or a citizen of the United States, at the time of the adoption of this Constitution, shall be eligible to the office of President; neither shall any person be eligible to that office who shall not have attained to the age of thirty-five years, and been fourteen years a resident within the United States.

5. In case of the removal of the President from office, or of his death, resignation, or inability to discharge the powers and duties of the said office, the same shall devolve on the Vice President, and the Congress may by law provide for the case of removal, death, resignation, or inability, both of the President and Vice President, declaring what officer shall then act as President, and such officer shall act accordingly, until the disability be removed, or a President shall be elected.

UNFORTUNATLY, THE LANGUAGE USED HERE CAUSED PROBLEMS OF HISTORICAL PROPORTIONS....

THE OPERATIVE PRECEDENT TOOK PLACE IN APRIL, 1841...

PRES. WILLIAM HENRY HARRISON TOOK OFFICE IN THE MIDDLE OF A RAGING BLIZZARD.

AT 68, HE MADE A 40-MINUTE SPEECH IN HIS SHIRTSLEEVES—OUTSIDE. HE DIED OF PNEUMONIA A MONTH LATER.

TWO DAYS AFTER PRES. HARRISON DIED, VICE-PRES. JOHN TYLER TOOK THE OATH OF OFFICE AS PRESIDENT.

NOBODY DOUBTED TYLER'S RIGHT TO TAKE OVER, BUT...

MANY **DID** OBJECT TO HIS USE OF THE TITLE, PERKS, AND MOST IMPORTANTLY, THE EXTRA **PAY**

WE'RE HERE TO SEE THE ACTING PRESIDENT

SLAM

SYNTAX ERROR. TRY AGAIN.

WHEN TYLER WAS ALMOST IMPEACHED IN 1843, IT WAS AS "VICE-PRESIDENT ACTING AS PRESIDENT." BUT TYLER WON HIS POINT. ON THE DEATHS OF THEIR PREDECESSORS, VICE-PRESIDENTS FILLMORE, JOHNSON (BOTH), ARTHUR, ROOSEVELT, COOLIDGE, AND TRUMAN BECAME PRESIDENT.

OKAY, THE VEEPEE BECOMES PRESIDENT IF THE PRESIDENT DIES. FINE. BUT WHAT IF HE'S COMATOSE FOR, LET'S SAY, SIX MONTHS. WHAT THEN?

THIS DISASTER TOOK PLACE IN THE FALL OF 1919, WHEN PRES. WILSON HAD A MASSIVE STROKE.

HE COULDN'T THINK. HE COULDN'T TALK. HE COULDN'T MOVE.

WHO WOULD RUN THE COUNTRY?

AFTER WILSON LEFT OFFICE IN 1921, THE MOVEMENT TO CORRECT THIS OVERSIGHT DIED. UNTIL THE 25th AMENDMENT WAS PASSED, THIS SORT OF THING COULD HAPPEN AGAIN. AND IT DID... (SEE P. 233)

6. The President shall, at stated times, receive for his services a compensation, which shall neither be increased nor diminished during the period for which he shall have been elected, and he shall not receive within that period any other emolument from the United States, or any of them.

7. Before he enter on the execution of his office, he shall take the following oath or affirmation—"I do solemnly swear (or affirm) that I will faithfully execute the office of President of the United States, and will to the best of my ability, preserve, protect and defend the Constitution of the United States."

1. The President shall be commander in chief of the army and navy of the United States, and of the militia of the several States, when called into the actual service of the United States;

THIS IS **NOT** AN HONORARY TITLE

IN 1794, DURING THE WHISKEY REBELLION PRES. WASHINGTON ACTUALLY LED HIS TROOPS INTO BATTLE!

ONWARD FOR GOD, AMERICA AND LITE BEER!

DURING WARTIME BEING COMMANDER-IN-CHIEF IS THE PRESIDENT'S MAIN FUNCTION. FOR INSTANCE, DURING THE CIVIL WAR, PRES. LINCOLN WENT OVER EVERYTHING HIS OFFICERS DID. IF THEY DIDN'T SHOW RESULTS QUICKLY, THEY WERE CANNED.

BOYS

AS HOLDER OF ULTIMATE MILITARY AUTHORITY, THE PRESIDENT IS THE ONLY ONE WHO CAN ORDER A NUCLEAR ATTACK. A SOBERING RESPONSIBILITY INDEED.

CAN'T YOU WAIT OUTSIDE FOR ONCE?

ESPECIALLY WHEN A PERSON WITH A SUITCASE FOLLOWS YOU WHEREVER YOU GO.

he may require the opinion, in writing of the principal officer
in each of the executive departments, upon any subject relating to
the duties of their respective offices,

and he shall have power to
grant reprieves and pardons for offenses against the United States,
except in cases of impeachment.

2. He shall have power, by and with the advice and consent of the Senate, to make treaties, provided two thirds of the senators present concur; and he shall nominate, and by and with the advice and consent of the Senate, shall appoint ambassadors, other public ministers and consuls, judges of the Supreme Court, and all other officers of the United States, whose appointments are not herein otherwise provided for, and which shall be established by law:

THE SENATE, AGAIN

WASHINGTON LEFT IN A HUFF, AND WITH ONE CEREMONIAL EXCEPTION, NO PRESIDENT HAS EVER RETURNED.

THIS DOESN'T MEAN THAT SENATORIAL ADVICE HAS NEVER BEEN SOLICITED SINCE THEN...

VERY MINOR JUDGESHIPS ARE SOMETHING PRESIDENTS NEITHER KNOW OR CARE ABOUT BUT HE HAS TO NOMINATE THEM ANYWAY.

WHERE THE HECK IS SCHLEPAVIC, MINNESOTA?

THE SENATORS FROM THE STATE IN QUESTION (ESPECIALLY IF THEY'RE FROM THE PRESIDENT'S PARTY) SEND THE PRESIDENT LISTS OF NAMES.

THIS IS KNOWN AS SENATORIAL COURTESY.

CONSENT IS A DIFFERENT MATTER.

80% OF THE TIME, SENATORIAL CONSENT IS GIVEN WITHOUT BATTING AN EYE. THE OTHER 20% ARE USUALLY BATTLES ROYAL, LASTING MONTHS (OR YEARS).

TREATIES NEED ⅔ OF THE SENATE IN ORDER TO RATIFY THEM. THIS IS BECAUSE THEY ARE, IN FACT, LAWS, AND THE HOUSE (MUCH TO ITS DISGUST) HAS NOTHING TO DO WITH THEM. IN THIS INSTANCE, IT IS THE PRESIDENT WHO DOES THE LEGISLATING AND THE SENATE HAS THE VETO.

LOOK, JOHN, I'VE JUST SIGNED A TREATY WITH PANAMA TO BUILD A CANAL!

BUT, MR. PRESIDENT, PANAMA ISN'T AN INDEPENDENT COUNTRY.

IT IS NOW!

the Congress may by law vest the appointment of such inferior officers, as they think proper, in the President alone, in the courts of law, or in the heads of departments

3. The President shall have power to fill up all vacancies that may happen during the recess of the Senate, by granting commissions which shall expire at the end of their next session.

IN AUG. 1795 PRES. WASHINGTON GAVE A RECESS APPOINTMENT TO JOHN RUTLEDGE TO BECOME CHIEF JUSTICE. THIS MEANT THAT HE GOT THE JOB FIRST AND HAD TO BE CONFIRMED LATER

*AT CONVENTION, SEE PAGE 37.

JOHN RUTLEDGE
JUDGE AND LUNATIC

THE SENATE DIDN'T LIKE (AMONG OTHER THINGS) THE FACT THAT DURING HIS TENURE AS AN ASSOCIATE JUSTICE HE HAD NEVER SHOWN UP FOR WORK! SO THEY REFUSED TO CONFIRM HIM IN DEC. 1795.

RUTLEDGE HAS THE UNIQUE DISTINCTION OF BEING THE ONLY PERSON **EVER** KICKED OFF THE SUPREME COURT

§3: LEADERSHIP

He shall from time to time give to the Congress information of the state of the Union, and recommend to their consideration such measures as he shall judge necessary and expedient;

EVERY YEAR (ALMOST) THE PRESIDENT ADDRESSES CONGRESS ON NATIONAL TELEVISION AND ASKS THEM TO PASS HIS PROGRAM.

...AND EVERY NOW AND THEN THEY DO!

he may, on extraordinary occasions, convene both Houses, or either of them, and in case of disagreement between them with respect to the time of adjournment, he may adjourn them to such time as he shall think proper;

AS IS USUAL IN AN ELECTION YEAR, THE REPUBLICANS COMPLAINED ABOUT THE DEMOCRATS AND MADE ALL SORTS OF PROMISES.

THAT GOSHDARN TRUMAN! IF ONLY HE'D GIVE US A CHANCE WE COULD REALLY DO SOMETHING!

KNOWING A GOOD STRAIGHT LINE WHEN HE SAW ONE, H.S.T. CALLED A SPECIAL SESSION IN LATE JULY.

AS TRUMAN EXPECTED, THE REPUBLICANS THEN PROCEEDED TO DO ABSOLUTELY NOTHING. LOSING MOST OF THEIR CREDIBILITY IN THE PROCESS.

OKAY, BUNKY, HERE'S YOUR CHANCE. DO SOMETHING.

CHICAGO TRIBUNE
DEWEY DEFEATS TRUMAN

NOT TO MENTION BOTH HOUSES OF CONGRESS.

he shall receive ambassadors and other public ministers;

AS FAR AS WE COULD TELL, THE ONLY AMBASSADOR FROM A LEGITIMATE GOVERNMENT THE PRESIDENT HAS REFUSED TO RECEIVE WAS NORA ASDORGA OF NICARAGUA IN 1984.

MAINLY BECAUSE SHE DIDN'T LIKE US OR WE DIDN'T LIKE HER OR...

I DON'T WANT TO GET INTO THIS RIGHT NOW SO LET'S JUST SKIP IT.

he shall take care that the laws be faithfully
executed, and shall commission all the officers of the United States.

*THIS, IN SUMMARY, IS THE PRESIDENT'S JOB.
...AND A HECK OF A DIFFICULT ONE IT IS, TOO...*

§4: IMPEACHMENT, YET AGAIN

The President, Vice President, and all civil officers of
the United States, shall be removed from office on impeachment
for, and conviction of, treason, bribery, or other high crimes and
misdemeanors.

THERE ARE TWO SCHOOLS OF THOUGHT ON THIS:

125

The judicial power of the United States shall be vested
in one Supreme Court, and in such inferior courts as the Congress
may from time to time ordain and establish.

§1 THE FEDERAL JUDICIARY SYSTEM

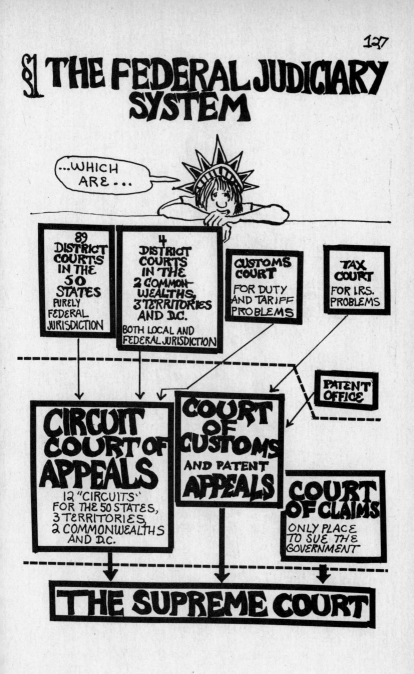

THEY CAN EITHER AFFIRM THE CONVICTION
OR REJECT IT.

IN EITHER CASE,
ONE OF THE JUDGES
WRITES DOWN THE
REASONS WHY IN A
REPORT CALLED AN
"OPINION."

I'M
HOT
TONIGHT.

AN APPELLATE COURT
JUDGE'S REPUTATION
RESTS ON HIS OPINIONS.

IF ONE JUDGE DISAGREES WITH THE OTHER
TWO, HE CAN WRITE A "DISSENT" EXPLAINING
WHY THEY WERE WRONG.

IF YOU WASH
OUT WITH THE
APPELLATE COURT,
DON'T WORRY...

THERE'S
ALWAYS THE
SUPREMES.

THE ONE SUPREME COURT (AS OPPOSED TO
DOZENS OF LOWER COURTS) IS THE COURT
OF LAST RESORT. IT HAS JURISDICTION
OVER EVERYTHING...

BOTH FEDERAL **AND** STATE COURTS.
IF YOU WASH OUT HERE, FORGET IT.

The judges, both of the Supreme and inferior courts, shall hold their offices during good behavior,

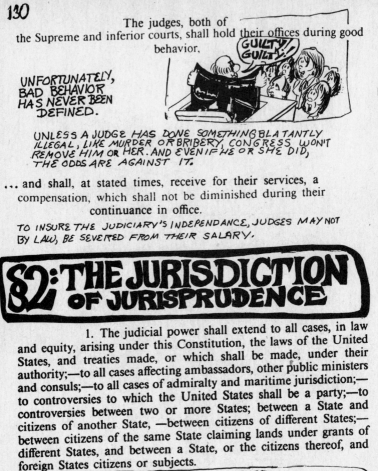

UNFORTUNATELY, BAD BEHAVIOR HAS NEVER BEEN DEFINED.

UNLESS A JUDGE HAS DONE SOMETHING BLATANTLY ILLEGAL, LIKE MURDER OR BRIBERY, CONGRESS WON'T REMOVE HIM OR HER. AND EVEN IF HE OR SHE DID, THE ODDS ARE AGAINST IT.

... and shall, at stated times, receive for their services, a compensation, which shall not be diminished during their continuance in office.

TO INSURE THE JUDICIARY'S INDEPENDANCE, JUDGES MAY NOT BY LAW, BE SEVERED FROM THEIR SALARY.

82: THE JURISDICTION OF JURISPRUDENCE

1. The judicial power shall extend to all cases, in law and equity, arising under this Constitution, the laws of the United States, and treaties made, or which shall be made, under their authority;—to all cases affecting ambassadors, other public ministers and consuls;—to all cases of admiralty and maritime jurisdiction;—to controversies to which the United States shall be a party;—to controversies between two or more States; between a State and citizens of another State, —between citizens of different States;—between citizens of the same State claiming lands under grants of different States, and between a State, or the citizens thereof, and foreign States citizens or subjects.

FEDERAL COURTS HAVE JURISDICTION OVER FEDERAL AND CONSTITUTIONAL LAW. PLUS INTERSTATE LAWSUITS. IN OTHER WORDS...

WE DON'T HANDLE PARKING TICKETS!

2. In all cases affecting ambassadors, other public ministers and consuls, and those in which a State shall be party, the Supreme Court shall have original jurisdiction. In all the other cases before mentioned, the Supreme Court shall have appellate jurisdiction, both as to law and to fact, with such exceptions, and under such regulations as the Congress shall make.

MARBURY v. MADISON

(1803, 1 CRANCH 137)

QUESTION: CAN TRULY GREAT MEN ACT LIKE DEMENTED FOUR-YEAR-OLDS AND GET AWAY WITH IT?

"JUSTICE OF THE PEACE" WILLIAM MARBURY

SECRETARY of STATE JAMES MADISON

MARCH 31, 1801 — 18 HOURS TILL THE **END OF THE WORLD!**... WELL, NOT EXACTLY, BUT THE NOTORIOUS VICE-PRESIDENT JEFFERSON WAS GOING TO TAKE OVER THE NATION, AND THAT WAS CLOSE ENOUGH FOR PRES. ADAMS!

SO HE WAS DOING THE ONLY THING HE COULD STILL DO TO SAVE THE NATION...

...APPOINT AS MANY JUDGES AS POSSIBLE.

JEFFERSON HAD ONLY BEEN ELECTED BECAUSE SAM SMITH PROMISED THAT T.J. WOULDN'T FIRE ANY FEDERALIST JUDGES (SEE P. 114).

HE WAS LYING THROUGH HIS TEETH, OF COURSE...

BUT THE FEDERALISTS DIDN'T KNOW THAT, SO THEY PASSED THE JUDICIARY ACT OF 1801.

THE JUDICIARY ACT WAS PASSED ON FEB. 13th. ADAMS THEN NOMINATED 42 JUSTICES OF THE PEACE FOR D.C., AND 16 APPEALS COURT JUDGES. THE LAME DUCK CONGRESS HAD QUICKLY CONFIRMED THEM, AS THEY WERE SURE THAT JEFFERSON WAS THE DEVIL.

THEN ADAMS FORMALLY APPOINTED THE NEW JUDICIARY BY SIGNING COMMISSIONS PREPARED BY SECRETARY OF STATE AND CHIEF JUSTICE SIMULTANEOUSLY JOHN MARSHALL

...WHO TAKES THEM BACK TO THE STATE DEPT.

JOHN MARSHALL (1755-1835) GREATEST CHIEF JUSTICE EVER.

12 HOURS ARE LEFT...

WITH THE AID OF CONGRESS, JEFFERSON HAD FIRED ALMOST ALL FEDERALIST JUDGES.

THOMAS JEFFERSON (1743-1826) WAS A GENIUS AND A STATESMAN, BUT HE WAS ALSO A POLITICIAN, AND COULD BE, ON OCCASION, A REAL S.O.B.

THE HEARING ITSELF WAS TOTALLY BIZARRE. THE CHIEF WITNESS FOR THE PROSECUTION WAS COUNSEL FOR THE DEFENSE, AND ONE OF THE JUDGES WAS MATERIALLY INVOLVED, HAVING BEEN THE CAUSE OF IT ALL.

MARSHALL AND HIS COLLEAGUES WERE IN A WELL-DESERVED BIND.

IF WE FIND FOR MADISON WE LOSE WHATEVER PRESTIGE WE HAVE LEFT.

...AND IF WE FIND FOR MARBURY CONGRESS HAS PROMISED TO HAVE US IMPEACHED.

DAMNED IF WE DO, DAMNED IF WE DON'T.

BUT, TO HIS EVERLASTING CREDIT, MARSHALL FOUND A THIRD WAY OUT OF HIS SELF-MADE BIND. HIS OPINION WENT SOMETHING LIKE THIS:

WE WOULD VERY MUCH LIKE TO ISSUE THE WRIT OF MANDAMUS, BECAUSE TOM JEFFERSON IS A JERK.

BUT THE LAW THAT GIVES US THE POWER TO DO SO IS UNCONSTITUTIONAL AND THEREFORE NULL AND VOID, SO WE CAN'T.

THE ABILITY TO DECLARE LAWS UNCONSTITUTIONAL IS THE MOST IMPORTANT POWER THE COURTS HAVE. WITHOUT IT AMERICA WOULDN'T EXIST, MUCH LESS AMERICAN FREEDOM.

3. The trial of all crimes, except in cases of impeachment, shall be by jury; and such trial shall be held in the State where the said crimes shall have been committed; but when not committed within any State, the trial shall be at such place or places as the Congress may by law have directed.

§3: TREASON!

1. Treason against the United States shall consist only in levying war against them, or in adhering to their enemies, giving them aid and comfort. No person shall be convicted of treason unless on the testimony of two witnesses to the same overt act, or on confession in open court.

2. The Congress shall have power to declare the punishment of treason, but no attainder of treason shall work corruption of blood, or forfeiture except during the life of the person attainted.

THIS IS HERE TO PROTECT LOYAL AMERICANS FROM THINGS LIKE...

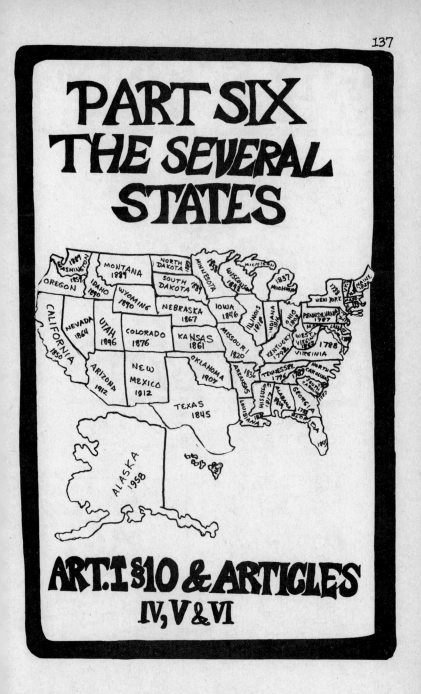

PART SIX
THE SEVERAL STATES

ART.I §10 & ARTICLES
IV, V & VI

ART. 1, §10: AN END TO INDEPENDENCE

WHEN A FOREIGN COUNTRY (LIKE TEXAS) JOINS THE UNION, IT LOSES CERTAIN POWERS THAT INDEPENDENT COUNTRIES HAVE.

FR'INSTANCE...

1. No State shall enter into any treaty, alliance, or confederation; grant letter of marque and reprisal; coin money; emit bills of credit; make anything but gold and silver coin a tender in payment of debts; pass any bill of attainder, *ex post facto* law, or law impairing the obligation of contracts, or grant any title of nobility. *THE BIT ABOUT IMPAIRING CONTRACTS WAS AT ONE TIME THE MOST IMPORTANT PART OF THE CONSTITUTION.*

CONTRACTS

A CONTRACT IS AN AGREEMENT BY TWO OR MORE PEOPLE (CORPORATIONS ARE LEGAL PERSONS) TO DO SOMETHING. IT IS LEGALLY BINDING, WHICH MEANS THAT YOU **HAVE** TO TO DO IT. FOR EXAMPLE:

JOHN PECK BUYS SOME LARGE TRACTS OF LAND FROM GEORGIA IN 1795.

PECK THEN SELLS IT TO ROBERT FLETCHER AT A LARGE PROFIT.

ALL WELL AND GOOD.

IT WAS THEN DISCOVERED THAT PECK AND HIS COMPATRIOTS HAD BRIBED SEVERAL STATE LEGISLATORS TO PUSH THE SALE THROUGH THE LEGISLATURE.

INDIGNANT, THE GEORGIA LEGISLATURE REPEALED THE SALE.

LEAVING POOR FLETCHER IN THE LURCH.

FLETCHER WAS AN INNOCENT VICTIM HERE. AND LIKE ANY GOOD INNOCENT VICTIM, HE DID HIS DUTY: HE SUED PECK.

SOB!

THE ISSUES IN THE CASE OF **FLETCHER v. PECK** (1809, 6 CRANCH 27) WERE QUITE SIMPLE: WAS THE ORIGINAL SALE LEGAL, AND IF IT WAS, COULD GEORGIA RENEG AFTER THE FACT?

CHIEF JUSTICE MARSHALL'S ANSWER WENT SOMETHING LIKE THIS:

1. JUST BECAUSE THE LEGISLATORS WERE BRIBED DOESN'T NULLIFY AN OTHERWISE PERFECTLY LEGAL ACT.
2. NO IT CAN'T. EVEN STATES HAVE TO LIVE UP TO THEIR OBLIGATIONS.

IN 1819, IN THE CASE OF **DARTMOUTH COLLEGE v. WOODWARD** (4 WHEATON 518) CORPORATE CHARTERS WERE DECLARED TO BE CONTRACTS UNDER THE LAW, AND THEREFORE IMMUNE FROM GOVERNMENT INTERFERENCE.

HOWEVER, IN HIS CONCURRING OPINION, ASSOC. JUSTICE JOSEPH STORY LEFT OPEN AN ESCAPE HATCH.

IF A STATE GOVERNMENT WISHES TO BE ABLE TO CHANGE A CORPORATE CHARTER AT WILL, JUST PUT IT IN THE FINE PRINT

REMEMBER, BEFORE SIGNING A CONTRACT **ALWAYS** READ THE FINE PRINT.

IF IT WASN'T FOR THE CONTRACT CLAUSE, LAWYERS WOULDN'T HAVE ANYTHING TO DO. THAT'S A FACT.

NOW WHERE WERE WE?

2. No State shall, without the consent of the Congress, lay any imposts or duties on imports or exports, except what may be absolutely necessary for executing its inspection laws: and the net produce of all duties and imposts laid by any State on imports or exports, shall be for the use of the treasury of the United States; and all such laws shall be subject to the revision and control of the Congress.

> THIS WAS PUT HERE SO THAT FLORIDA WON'T DO TO MISSISSIPPI WHAT JAPAN IS DOING TO US. THE INDIVIDUAL STATES CAN, HOWEVER, INSPECT INCOMING MERCHANDISE TO MAKE SURE THERE AREN'T ANY WEIRD BUGS.

3. No State shall, without the consent of the Congress, lay any duty of tonnage, keep troops, or ships of war in time of peace, enter into any agreement or compact with another State, or with a foreign power, or engage in war, unless actually invaded, or in such imminent danger as will not admit of delay.

THE LAST WORD ON THIS SUBJECT IS STILL PENDING.

ARTICLE IV: INTERSTATE RELATIONS

§1: FULL FAITH & CREDIT

Full faith and credit shall be given in each State to the public acts, records, and judicial proceedings of every other State. And the Congress may by general laws prescribe the manner in which such acts, records and proceedings shall be proved, and the effect thereof.

§2: PRIVILEGES, RIGHTS & IMMUNITIES

1. The citizens of each State shall be entitled to all privileges and immunities of citizens in the several States.

THIS WAS ONE OF THE ONLY PARTS OF THE CONSTITUTION TO BE DECLARED UNCONSTITUTIONAL...

THE CASE:

CORFIELD V. CORYELL (1823)

(6 FED CASES 546, 550)

ONE OF THE BIGGIES

BARRON v. BALTIMORE

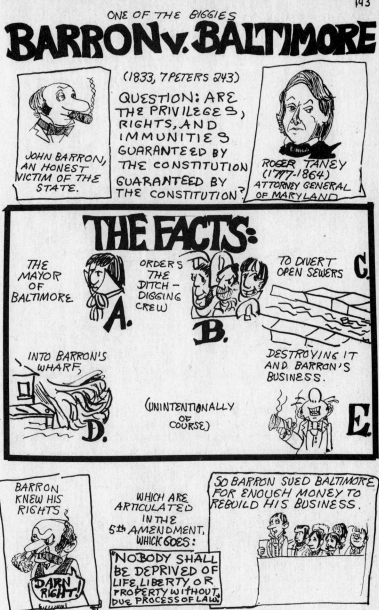

(1833, 7 PETERS 243)

QUESTION: ARE THE PRIVILEGES, RIGHTS, AND IMMUNITIES GUARANTEED BY THE CONSTITUTION GUARANTEED BY THE CONSTITUTION?

JOHN BARRON, AN HONEST VICTIM OF THE STATE.

ROGER TANEY (1777-1864) ATTORNEY GENERAL OF MARYLAND

THE FACTS:

THE MAYOR OF BALTIMORE **A.**

ORDERS THE DITCH-DIGGING CREW **B.**

TO DIVERT OPEN SEWERS **C.**

INTO BARRON'S WHARF, **D.**

(UNINTENTIONALLY OF COURSE)

DESTROYING IT AND BARRON'S BUSINESS. **E.**

BARRON KNEW HIS RIGHTS

DARN RIGHT!

WHICH ARE ARTICULATED IN THE 5th AMENDMENT, WHICH GOES:

"NOBODY SHALL BE DEPRIVED OF LIFE, LIBERTY OR PROPERTY WITHOUT DUE PROCESS OF LAW"

SO BARRON SUED BALTIMORE FOR ENOUGH MONEY TO REBUILD HIS BUSINESS.

BUT BALTIMORE APPEALED, AND IT WON THERE!

THERE WAS ONLY ONE AVENUE LEFT:
THE SUPREME COURT!

CHIEF JUSTICE
MARSHALL'S
OPINION WENT
LIKE THIS:

THE FIRST AMENDMENT
TO THE CONSTITUTION
SAYS: "CONGRESS SHALL
PASS NO LAW!" THEREFORE
THE IMMUNITIES ARTICULATED
IN THE FIFTH AMENDMENT
DO NOT APPLY TO THE
STATES, ONLY TO THE
FEDERAL GOVERNMENT.

THIS WAS
MARSHALL'S
LAST OPINION.
IT WAS ALSO
HIS WORST.

IT WOULD TAKE A
CIVIL WAR, **THREE**
CONSTITUTIONAL AMENDMENTS,
AND 130 YEARS OF STRUGGLE
BEFORE ART 4 §2 WOULD
BE PUT BACK IN THE
CONSTITUTION.

2. A person charged in any State with treason, felony, or other crime, who shall flee from justice, and be found in another State, shall on demand of the executive authority of the State from which he fled, be delivered up to be removed to the State having jurisdiction of the crime.

IN HIS OPINION IN THE
CASE OF **KENTUCKY** v.
DENNISON (1861, 24 HOWARD 66)
CHIEF JUSTICE ROGER B. TANEY
DECLARED THAT THIS WAS
ONLY AN UNENFORCEABLE
SUGGESTION.

BUT DON'T
WORRY, IN
1862 CONGRESS
PASSED A
LAW MAKING
CROSSING
STATE LINES
TO AVOID
ARREST
ILLEGAL.

ALL STATES HONOR EXTRADITION REQUESTS. IT'S TOO DANGEROUS NOT TO.

3. No person held to service or labor in one State under the laws thereof, escaping into another, shall in consequence of any law or regulation therein, be discharged from such service or labor, but shall be delivered up on claim of the party to whom such service or labor may be due.

THIS HAS TO DO WITH RUNAWAY SLAVES, SO WE'LL IGNORE IT.

§3: NEW STATES

1. New States may be admitted by the Congress into this Union; but no new State shall be formed or erected within the jurisdiction of any other State, nor any State be formed by the junction of two or more States, or parts of States, without the consent of the legislatures of the States concerned as well as of the Congress.

WRONG!

WEST VIRGINIA WAS TORN OUT OF VIRGINIA AGAINST THE LATTER'S WILL IN 1863.

OF COURSE, THEY WERE AT WAR WITH US AT THE TIME, BUT HEY, IT COUNTS, RIGHT?

AND NO STATE LEGISLATURE IN ITS RIGHT MIND WOULD CONSENT TO A **MERGER** ONCE A STATE IS LET IN, IT IS ON EQUAL TERMS WITH THE OTHERS.

2. The Congress shall have power to dispose of and make all needful rules and regulations respecting the territory or other property belonging to the United States; and nothing in this Constitution shall be so construed as to prejudice any claims of the United States, or of any particular State.

THIS ALLOWS CONGRESS TO EXERCISE POWERS NORMALLY RESERVED FOR THE STATES WHILE A CANDIDATE FOR MEMBERSHIP WAITS TO BE LET IN.

MEMBERS ONLY

NEXT

§4·REPUBLICAN FORMS OF GOVERNMENT

The United States shall guarantee to every State in this Union a republican form of government, and shall protect each of them against invasion; and on application of the legislature, or of the executive (when the legislature cannot be convened) against domestic violence.

ARTICLE V: THE AMENDMENT PROCESS

The Congress, whenever two thirds of both Houses shall deem it necessary, shall propose amendements to this Constitution, or, on the application of the legislature of two thirds of the several States, shall call a convention for proposing amendments, which in either case, shall be valid to all intents and purposes, as part of this Constitution when ratified by the legislatures of three fourths of the several States, or by conventions in three fourths thereof, as the one or the other mode of ratification may be proposed by the Congress; Provided that no amendment which may be made prior to the year one thousand eight hundred and eight shall in any manner affect the first and fourth clauses in the ninth section of the first article; and that no State, without its consent, shall be deprived of its equal suffrage in the Senate.

148

BUT WHAT ABOUT STATES CALLING FOR A SECOND CONSTITUTIONAL CONVENTION?

IN 1962 ENOUGH STATES PETITIONED TO CALL ONE TO REPEAL (OR GUT) THE INCOME TAX.

IT WAS IGNORED

IT'LL NEVER HAPPEN.

THERE IS NO REASON TO BELIEVE THAT CONGRESS WON'T IGNORE THE NEXT ONE (BALANCED BUDGET, WE THINK) TOO.

ARTICLE VI: DEBT, RANK & SWEARING

1. All debts contracted and engagements entered into, before the adoption of this Constitution, shall be as valid against the United States under this Constitution, as under the Confederation.

A RESPONSIBLE GOVERNMENT DOES **NOT** START OFF BY SAYING IT'S NOT GOING TO PAY ITS DEBTS

ESPECIALLY WHEN FOREIGN POWERS WERE PLANNING TO FORECLOSE!

2. This Constitution, and the laws of the United States which shall be made in pursuance thereof; and all treaties made, or which shall be made, under the authority of the United States, shall be the supreme law of the land; and the Judges in every State shall be bound thereby, anything in the Constitution or laws of any State to the contrary notwithstanding.

THE REASON WHY THE UNITED STATES OF AMERICA STILL EXISTS AFTER 200+ YEARS IS BECAUSE THE CONSTITUTION EXPLAINS WHO'S BOSS — IT IS! FOR INSTANCE...

McCULLOGH v. MARYLAND

FOR ALL YOU LETTER CARRIERS OUT THERE WHO ARE WONDERING WHY YOU STILL HAVE TO PAY STATE INCOME TAX, YES, THERE IS A REASON.

CONGRESS MADE YOUR SALARIES TAXABLE BY ANYBODY. SORRY ABOUT THAT.

3. The senators and representatives before mentioned, and the members of the several State legislatures, and all executive and judicial officers, both of the United States and of the several States, shall be bound by oath or affirmation to support this Constitution; but no religious test shall ever be required as a qualification to any office or public trust under the United States.

THAT'S WHAT A MR. TORASCO THOUGHT WHEN THEY ASKED HIM TO TAKE ONE WHEN HE APPLIED TO BECOME A NOTARY PUBLIC IN MARYLAND.

AND THE SUPREME COURT AGREED. HIS RIGHTS WERE VIOLATED.

SPEAKING OF WHICH...

THE BILL OF RIGHTS: AMENDMENTS 1–10 (1791)

GUILT

CAN BE A GREAT INSPIRATION.

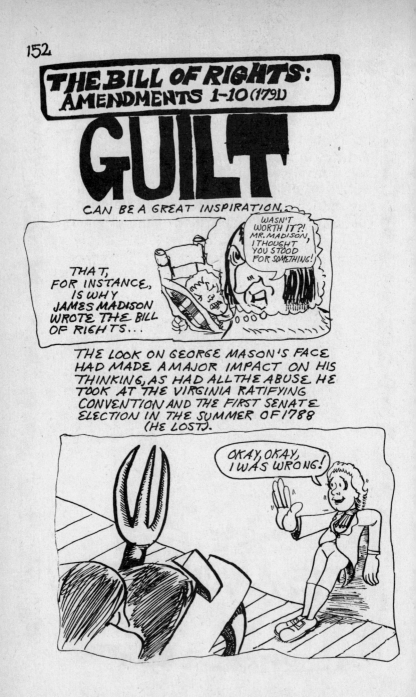

THAT, FOR INSTANCE, IS WHY JAMES MADISON WROTE THE BILL OF RIGHTS...

WASN'T WORTH IT?! MR. MADISON, I THOUGHT YOU STOOD FOR SOMETHING!

THE LOOK ON GEORGE MASON'S FACE HAD MADE A MAJOR IMPACT ON HIS THINKING, AS HAD ALL THE ABUSE HE TOOK AT THE VIRGINIA RATIFYING CONVENTION AND THE FIRST SENATE ELECTION IN THE SUMMER OF 1788 (HE LOST).

OKAY, OKAY, I WAS WRONG!

AFTER SEVERAL MONTHS OF TRYING TO IGNORE THEM, THE HOUSE PASSED ALL SEVENTEEN. THE SENATE THEN MERGED FIVE AMENDMENTS INTO TWO AND CLEANED UP THE LANGUAGE IN THE REST

...EXCEPT 2.

WHERE'S THE ONE PROTECTING SPEECH, THE PRESS AND PEACEFUL ASSEMBLY FROM THE STATES?

IT WAS REDUNDANT. ART. IV §2 OF THE CONSTITUTION SAYS PRETTY MUCH THE SAME THING.

I HOPE YOU'RE RIGHT.

(THE ONE PROTECTING US FROM BUREAUCRATS WAS DEEMED UNNECESSARY—LITTLE DID THEY KNOW!)

THE 12 REVISED AMENDMENTS WERE SENT TO THE STATES IN SEPTEMBER, 1789.

UNLIKE THE ORIGINAL CONSTITUTION, THE FIRST 12 AMENDMENTS TOOK 2½ YEARS TO BE RATIFIED... AND NOT ALL OF THEM MADE IT.

IN CONGRESS

THE FIRST TWO AMENDMENTS FAILED, SO ARTICLE III OF THE BILL OF RIGHTS IS NOW THE FIRST AMENDMENT.

(HOWEVER, WE'LL CALL IT ARTICLE III, OR THE FIRST AMENDMENT—DEPENDING ON HOW WE FEEL.)

THE REMAINING TEN BECAME PART OF THE CONSTITUTION IN DECEMBER, 1791.

ARTICLE I
Congress shall make no law...

... respecting an establishment of religion, or prohibiting the free exercise thereof; or abridging the freedom of speech, or of the press; or the right of the people peaceably to assemble, and to petition the government for a redress of grievances.

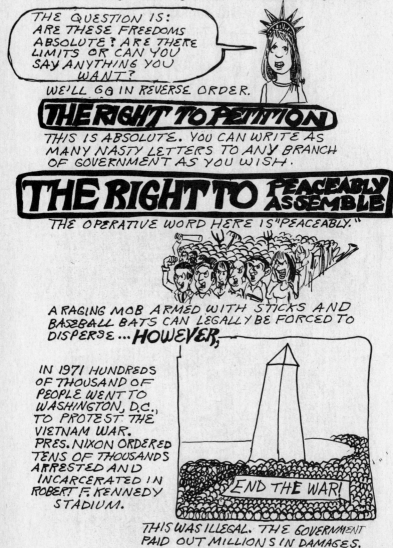

THE QUESTION IS: ARE THESE FREEDOMS ABSOLUTE? ARE THERE LIMITS OR CAN YOU SAY ANYTHING YOU WANT?

WE'LL GO IN REVERSE ORDER.

THE RIGHT TO PETITION

THIS IS ABSOLUTE. YOU CAN WRITE AS MANY NASTY LETTERS TO ANY BRANCH OF GOVERNMENT AS YOU WISH.

THE RIGHT TO PEACEABLY ASSEMBLE

THE OPERATIVE WORD HERE IS "PEACEABLY."

A RAGING MOB ARMED WITH STICKS AND BASEBALL BATS CAN LEGALLY BE FORCED TO DISPERSE ... HOWEVER,

IN 1971 HUNDREDS OF THOUSAND OF PEOPLE WENT TO WASHINGTON, D.C., TO PROTEST THE VIETNAM WAR. PRES. NIXON ORDERED TENS OF THOUSANDS ARRESTED AND INCARCERATED IN ROBERT F. KENNEDY STADIUM.

END THE WAR!

THIS WAS ILLEGAL. THE GOVERNMENT PAID OUT MILLIONS IN DAMAGES.

FREEDOM OF EXPRESSION

THERE IS ONE POLITICAL STATEMENT EVERYBODY IN THE WORLD CAN MAKE:

LONG LIVE GOVERNMENT!

BUT IS THAT ALL THERE IS TO FREE SPEECH?

YES!

ANYONE CRITICIZING PRES. ADAMS OR THE FEDERALIST PARTY COULD WIND UP IN JAIL FOR UP TO TWO YEARS.

SAID PRES. JOHN ADAMS AS HE SIGNED **THE SEDITION ACT OF 1798.**

REACTION WAS SWIFT. THE LEGISLATURES OF BOTH KENTUCKY AND VIRGINIA DECLARED THE LAW UNCONSTITUTIONAL AND VOID, SETTING A VERY UNFORTUNATE PRECEDENT.

IN THE 1800 ELECTION ADAMS CAME IN THIRD.

THUD

THE SEDITION LAW EXPIRED IN 1801 AND PRES. JEFFERSON PARDONED THE VICTIMS.

FOR THE NEXT 116 YEARS THE GOVERNMENT BEHAVED ITSELF

EVEN DURING THE CIVIL WAR.

...THEN CAME WORLD WAR ONE!!

100 THOUSAND PEOPLE WERE KILLED IN LESS THAN 18 MONTHS.

WE MUST MAKE YOU SAFE FOR DEMOCRACY, HEE! HEE HEE!

CONGRESS PASSED THE ESPIONAGE ACT OF 1917 AND THE SEDITION ACT OF 1918, WHICH TEMPORARILY TURNED THE FIRST AMENDMENT INTO TOILET PAPER.

ANYBODY CRITICIZING WORLD WAR ONE COULD GO TO JAIL FOR 20 YEARS.

THE NEW YORK TIMES WAS BANNED FROM THE MAILS! GOOD AMERICANS WENT TO JAIL FOR WRITING ARTICLES AND MAKING SPEECHES! THIS FORCED THE SUPREME COURT TO OPINE ON THE LIMITS (IF ANY) ON FREEDOM OF SPEECH AND THE PRESS.

SCHENCK v. U.S. (1919)

(249 U.S. 47)

SCHENCK WAS CONVICTED OF SENDING OUT SUBVERSIVE JUNK MAIL. WHEN THE CASE GOT TO THE SUPREME COURT, THE LATTER GAVE THE SEMI-DEFINITIVE PRONOUNCEMENT ON THE LIMITS OF FREE SPEECH.

WE ADMIT THAT IN MANY PLACES AND IN ORDINARY TIMES WHAT THE DEFENDANT SAID WOULD BE WELL WITHIN HIS CONSTITUTIONAL RIGHTS.

BUT THE CHARACTER OF THE ACT DEPENDS ON THE CIRCUMSTANCES IN WHICH IT IS DONE. EVEN THE MOST STRINGENT PROTECTION OF FREE SPEECH WOULDN'T PROTECT A MAN FROM FALSELY SHOUTING "FIRE!" IN A THEATER, CAUSING A PANIC.

THE QUESTION IS WHETHER THE WORDS POSE A CLEAR AND PRESENT DANGER, BRINGING SUBSTANTIVE EVILS TO COME ABOUT.

WHILE IT MAY **SOUND** LOGICAL, THIS POSES SOME HEAVY PROBLEMS, LIKE, HOW DO YOU TELL A CLEAR AND PRESENT DANGER FROM A FUZZY AND POSSIBLE ONE?

THIS HAS BEEN TROUBLING THE GOVERNMENT AND THE COURTS FOR NIGH ON 70 YEARS.

USUALLY AND (FORTUNATELY) THE GOVERNMENT LOSES. THERE ARE TWO DEFINITIVE RULINGS ON FREEDOM OF EXPRESSION AS PROTECTED BY THE FIRST AMENDMENT PROPER.

HANNEGAN v. ESQUIRE, INC.

(1946, 327 U.S. 146)

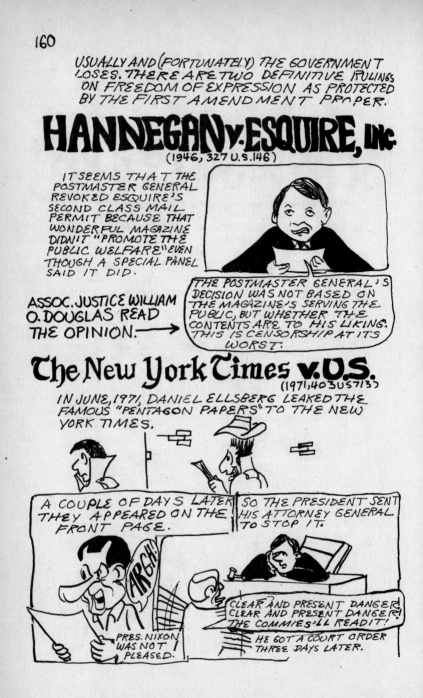

IT SEEMS THAT THE POSTMASTER GENERAL REVOKED ESQUIRE'S SECOND CLASS MAIL PERMIT BECAUSE THAT WONDERFUL MAGAZINE DIDN'T "PROMOTE THE PUBLIC WELFARE" EVEN THOUGH A SPECIAL PANEL SAID IT DID.

ASSOC. JUSTICE WILLIAM O. DOUGLAS READ THE OPINION. →

THE POSTMASTER GENERAL'S DECISION WAS NOT BASED ON THE MAGAZINE'S SERVING THE PUBLIC, BUT WHETHER THE CONTENTS ARE TO HIS LIKING. THIS IS CENSORSHIP AT ITS WORST.

The New York Times v. U.S.

(1971, 403 U.S. 713)

IN JUNE, 1971, DANIEL ELLSBERG LEAKED THE FAMOUS "PENTAGON PAPERS" TO THE NEW YORK TIMES.

A COUPLE OF DAYS LATER THEY APPEARED ON THE FRONT PAGE.

SO THE PRESIDENT SENT HIS ATTORNEY GENERAL TO STOP IT.

ARGH!

PRES. NIXON WAS NOT PLEASED.

CLEAR AND PRESENT DANGER! CLEAR AND PRESENT DANGER! THE COMMIES'LL READ IT!

HE GOT A COURT ORDER THREE DAYS LATER.

NO SOONER HAD THE TIMES BEEN ENJOINED WHEN THE WASHINGTON POST BEGAN PUBLISHING,

THEN THE MIAMI HERALD...

THEN THE CHICAGO TRIBUNE.

THE CASE FINALLY GOT TO THE SUPREME COURT AT THE END OF THE MONTH. JUSTICE DOUGLAS'S OPINION WENT LIKE THIS:

IT SHOULD BE NOTED THAT THE FIRST AMENDMENT STATES THAT...

CONGRESS SHALL PASS NO LAW... ABRIDGING FREEDOM OF SPEECH OR OF THE PRESS. THAT LEAVES NO ROOM FOR GOVERNMENT RESTRAINT OF THE PRESS.

AND THAT, AS THEY SAY, IS THAT.

FREEDOM OF RELIGION

NOW ABOUT ESTABLISHMENT OF RELIGION... THE GOVERNMENT HAS BEEN VERY GOOD ABOUT THIS...

..THEY HAVEN'T EVEN TRIED.

THE CONGRESSIONAL PRAYER SERVICES DON'T COUNT. (BECAUSE YOU DON'T HAVE TO SHOW UP.)

BUT WHAT ABOUT FREEDOM OF WORSHIP?

O LORD, PLEASE KEEP THE MAJORITY AND MINORITY LEADERS FROM BEATING EACH OTHER UP AGAIN. AMEN.

OWA, TAGU, SIAM

CAN THE GOVERNMENT LIMIT THAT?

IN THE CASE OF REYNOLDS V. U.S. (1878, 98 US 135) (IT INVOLVED A MORMON FELLOW ARRESTED FOR HAVING TWO WIVES), CHIEF JUSTICE MORRISON WAITE GAVE THE DEFINITIVE OPINION ON THE SUBJECT...

WHILE CONGRESS IS DEPRIVED OF ALL POWER TO REGULATE BELIEF, IT CAN REGULATE ACTIONS THAT ARE SUBVERSIVE TO THE SOCIAL ORDER.

SUPPOSE ONE BELIEVED THAT HUMAN SACRIFICE WAS A NECESSARY PART OF RELIGIOUS WORSHIP. COULD IT BE SERIOUSLY CONSIDERED THAT THE CIVIL GOVERNMENT COULDN'T INTERFERE? I THINK NOT.

BIGAMY AND HUMAN SACRIFICE, THAT'S ABOUT IT.

ARTICLE II

A well regulated militia, being necessary to the security of a free State, the right of the people to keep and bear arms, shall not be infringed.

THE OPERATIVE PHRASE HERE IS "WELL REGULATED MILITIA,"

ASSOC. JUSTICE JOSEPH STORY PUT IT THIS WAY:

HOW IS IT PRACTICABLE TO KEEP THE PEOPLE DULY ARMED WITHOUT SOME SORT OF ORGANIZATION?

THAT IS WHY THE STATES AND LOCALITIES HAVE SET UP THOUSANDS OF WELL REGULATED MILITIAS.

EXCEPT THAT NOWADAYS THEY'RE CALLED "POLICE DEPARTMENTS."

DROP IT, BUSTER!

WELL REGULATED ALSO MEANS THAT GUN CONTROL IS AN ABSOLUTE NECESSITY (SORRY, NATIONAL RIFLE ASSOCIATION).

ARTICLE III

No soldier shall, in time of peace be quartered in any house, without the consent of the owner, nor in time of war, but in a manner to be prescribed by law.

ARTICLE IV

The right of the people to be secure in the persons, houses, papers, and effects, against unreasonable searches and seizures, shall not be violated, and no warrants shall issue, but upon probable cause, supported by oath or affirmation, and particularly describing the place to be searched, and the persons or things to be seized.

IT WORKS SOMETHING LIKE THIS:

THE CASE:

AGNELLO v. U.S.
(1925, 269 U.S. 20)

THE FEDS DIDN'T HAVE A WARRANT.

ALBA AND AGNELLO WERE CONVICTED, MAINLY ON THE ILLEGALLY OBTAINED EVIDENCE.

SINCE HE WAS BUSTED BY **FEDERAL** AGENTS, THE FOURTH AMENDMENT CAME INTO PLAY. THIS WAS THE BASIS FOR THE APPEAL.

ASSOC. JUSTICE PIERCE BUTLER READ THE OPINION:

WARRANTLESS BREAK-INS ARE BANNED BY THE 4th AMENDMENT. SO FEDERAL AGENTS HAD NO RIGHT TO PERFORM ONE.

IF THE GOVERNMENT BREAKS THE LAW, THE FRUITS OF ITS CRIME MAY NOT BE USED IN COURT.

IN OTHER WORDS, THE LAW MUST OBEY THE LAW.

ARTICLE V

No person shall be held to answer for a capital, or otherwise infamous crime, unless on a presentment or indictment of a grand jury, except in cases arising in the land or naval forces, or in the militia, when in actual service in time of war or public danger;

GRAND JURIES AND COURTS MARTIAL

FIRST, SOME DEFINITIONS:

CAPITAL CRIME: ONE FOR WHICH THE PUNISHMENT IS **DEATH**.

INFAMOUS CRIME: ANY THAT CAN LAND YOU IN JAIL.

GRAND JURY: A GROUP OF CITIZENS IMPANELED BY THE COURTS TO INVESTIGATE A CRIME AND CHARGE (INDICT) PEOPLE WITH IT.

ALL FINE AND DANDY, BUT WHAT ABOUT THAT EXCEPTION ABOUT THE MILITARY? JUST WHO IS INCLUDED?

I MEAN BESIDES SOLDIERS AND SAILORS.

EX·PARTE MILLIGAN

(1866, 4 WALLACEZ)

ON OCT. 5, 1864 LAMBDEN P. MILLIGAN WAS ARRESTED FOR **CONSPIRACY.** HE WAS TRIED BY A MILITARY TRIBUNAL AND SENTENCED TO **DEATH!**

BEING A LAWYER, MILLIGAN IMMEDIATELY DEMANDED A WRIT OF HABEAS CORPUS, WHICH HE DIDN'T GET, BECAUSE IT WAS SUSPENDED.

AND BESIDES HE WAS GUILTY! BUYING GUNS ISN'T TALK!

WHILE MILLIGAN'S REQUEST WAFTED ITS WAY THROUGH THE COURTS, THE WAR ENDED AND PRES. ANDREW JOHNSON COMMUTED MILLIGAN'S SENTENCE TO LIFE. THE REQUEST GOT TO THE SUPREME COURT IN APRIL, 1866.

THE MAIN ISSUE HERE ISN'T MR. MILLIGAN'S LOYALTY...

BUT HIS RIGHTS

YOU CANNOT COURT MARTIAL A CIVILIAN EXCEPT IN A WAR ZONE.

AND YOUR HONORS...

THE SUPREME COURT AGREED. ASSOC. JUSTICE DAVID DAVIS READ THE OPINION:

WE ARE REVERSING HIS CONVICTION. THE FIFTH AMENDMENT PROHIBITS THE COURT MARTIAL OF CIVILIANS WHEN A CIVIL TRIAL IN NORMAL COURTS IS READILY AVAILABLE.

INDIANA WAS NEVER AT ANY TIME A WAR ZONE!

UNLIKE HABEAS CORPUS, THE BILL OF RIGHTS MAY NOT BE SUSPENDED.

nor shall any person be subject for the same offense to be twice put in jeopardy of life or limb;

U.S. v. SANGES
(1892, 144 U.S. 310)

THE PROSECUTION APPEALED. BUT THE SUPREME COURT THEN SAID THAT THE PROSECUTION COULD *NEVER* APPEAL AN AQUITTAL—DOUBLE JEOPARDY.

... nor shall be compelled in any criminal case to be a witness against himself,

DOUBTLESS YOU'VE HEARD OF TAKING THE FIFTH. THE IMMUNITY FROM SELF-INCRIMINATION PROTECTS US FROM:

OR WORSE... ZIANG SUNWAN v. U.S.

(1924, 266 U.S.1)

NEW YORK CITY, FEB. 1, 1919, WASHINGTON, D.C. POLICE ENTER THE MODEST LODGINGS OF ZIANG SUNWAN.

AFTER THEY SEARCH HIS ROOM (WITHOUT A WARRANT, OF COURSE,) ZIANG "CONSENTS" TO ACCOMPANY THEM BACK TO D.C.

OH, YEAH, WE FORGOT TO MENTION THAT ZIANG WAS EXTREMLY ILL, HAVING BOTH SPASTIC COLITIS (A VERY PAINFUL BLOCKAGE IN THE INTESTINES) AND THE KILLER FLU OF 1919!

WHICH WAS WHY, OF COURSE, HE WAS REFUSED MEDICAL ATTENTION (EXCEPT FOR A SHORT VISIT FROM A POLICE SURGEON, WHO DID NOTHING).

CONFESS!

FOR THE NEXT EIGHT DAYS, ZIANG WAS INTERROGATED WITHOUT MERCY FOR UP TO 18 HOURS A DAY!

OW! OW! OW!

EVERY DAY HE GOT SICKER AND SICKER.

ON THE EIGHTH DAY HE WAS TAKEN TO THE SCENE OF THE CRIME AND INTERROGATED FOR TEN HOURS.

THERE! THAT'S WHERE YOU KILLED HIM!

UHHH...

THEY THEN TOOK HIM BACK TO THE POLICE STATION, AND WORKING IN 8-HOUR SHIFTS, CONTINUED THE QUESTIONING FOR TWO DAYS STRAIGHT.

ON THE ELEVENTH DAY, ZIANG, NOW BOTH A MENTAL AND PHYSICAL WRECK, SIGNS THE CONFESSION. ONLY THEN WAS A DOCTOR LET IN.

BASED ON THIS "CONFESSION," ZIANG WAS CONVICTED OF MURDER AND SENTENCED TO HANG. SINCE D.C. IS A FEDERAL ENCLAVE, THE FIFTH AMENDMENT WAS EFFECTIVE.

ASSOC. JUSTICE LOUIS BRANDEIS READ THE OPINION:

A CONFESSION IS VOLUNTARY IN LAW ONLY IF IT IS IN FACT VOLUNTARILY MADE. THIS WASN'T.

THIS IS WHY COPS HATE THE SUPREME COURT.

... nor be deprived of life, liberty, or property, without due process of law;

DUE PROCESS OF LAW? JUST WHAT SORT OF LEGAL PROCESS IS DUE AN ACCUSED PERSON?

WELL, IT ALL DEPENDS ON THE CRIME.

PARKING TICKETS REQUIRE VERY LITTLE. EVERYTHING ELSE REQUIRES A GRAND JURY INVESTIGATION, A FAIR TRIAL AND AS MANY APPEALS AS ONE CAN POSSIBLY GET.

... nor shall private property be taken for public use without just compensation.

IF THERE IS A WAR IN YOUR BACK YARD, YOU CAN CHARGE RENT.

ARTICLE VI

In all criminal prosecutions, the accused shall enjoy the right to a speedy and public trial, by an impartial jury of the State and district wherein the crime shall have been committed, which district shall have been previously ascertained by law, and to be informed of the nature and cause of the accusation; to be confronted with the witnesses against him; to have compulsory process for obtaining witness in his favor, and to have the assistance of counsel for his defense.

THIS IS THE VERY ESSENCE OF A FAIR TRIAL.

ARTICLE VII

In suits at common law, where the value in controversy shall exceed twenty dollars, the right of trial by jury shall be preserved, and no fact tried by a jury shall be otherwise reexamined in any court of the United States, than according to the rules of the common law

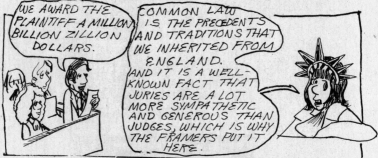

ARTICLE VIII

Excessive bail shall not be required, nor excessive fines imposed, nor cruel and unusual punishments inflicted.

ARTICLE IX

The enumeration in the Constitution of certain rights shall not be construed to deny or disparage others retained by the people.

ARTICLE X

The powers not delegated to the United States by the Constitution, nor prohibited by it to the States, are reserved to the States respectively, or to the people.

IN OTHER WORDS, EACH INDIVIDUAL STATE AND LOCALITY HAS THE RIGHT TO RUN ITS OWN INTERNAL AFFAIRS WITHOUT MUCH INTERFERENCE FROM WASHINGTON.

IT USED TO BE THAT MOST STATE GOVERNMENTS FIRMLY BELIEVED THAT THE FEDERAL GOVERNMENT HAD NO RIGHT TO INTERFERE IN THEIR INTERNAL AFFAIRS WHATSOEVER.

WELCOME TO YANKEE GO HOME

THIS LED TO PROBLEMS.

ESPECIALLY WHEN IT CAME TO CIVIL RIGHTS.

BY THE 1950'S STATES' RIGHTS HAD BECOME A SYNONYM FOR RACISM

STATES' RIGHTS STATES' RIGHTS

NOTHING WAS AS DEAR TO SOME STATE GOVERNMENTS AS THE "RIGHT" TO TYRANNIZE THEIR MINORITIES.

THE TENTH AMENDMENT AT ONE TIME OR ANOTHER HAS COME INTO CONFLICT WITH THE SUPREMACY CLAUSE (ART.6 §2) AND THE COMMERCE CLAUSE (ART.1 §8), AND ALMOST COMPLETELY RUINED THE PRIVILEGES AND IMMUNITIES CLAUSE (ART. 4 §2). SOMETIMES IT PREVAILED AND SOMETIMES IT DIDN'T.

10.

FLOAT LIKE A BUTTERFLY, STING LIKE A BEE!..

BUT MOSTLY IT CAME INTO CONFLICT WITH THE CIVIL WAR AMENDMENTS

AND THAT'S A TALE IN ITSELF. BUT FIRST...

THE ELEVENTH AMENDMENT (1795)

THE ELEVENTH AMENDMENT IS ONE OF THE LEAST UNDERSTANDABLE AND LEAST IMPORTANT OF THE BUNCH. FOR ONE THING, IT IS TOTALLY PROCEDURAL AND HAS NOTHING TO DO WITH FREEDOM PER SE. BUT IT DOES ANSWER AN INTERESTING QUESTION: HOW DO YOU SUE A STATE?

THE CASE:

CHISHOLM v. GEORGIA (1793-95)

(2 DALLAS 431)

THE PLAINTIFF:

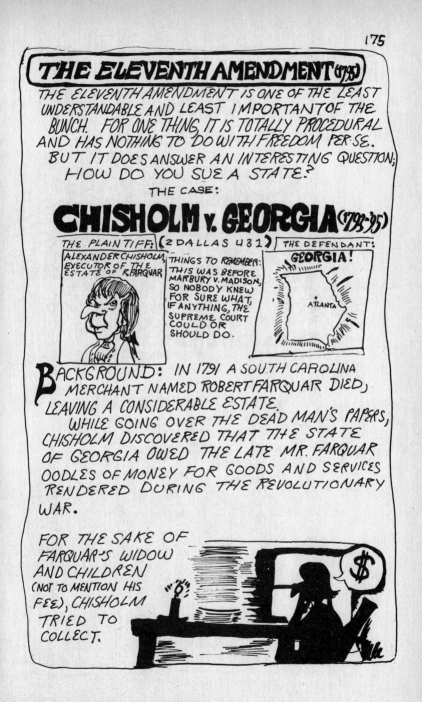

ALEXANDER CHISHOLM, EXECUTOR OF THE ESTATE OF R. FARQUAR

THINGS TO REMEMBER: THIS WAS BEFORE MARBURY V. MADISON, SO NOBODY KNEW FOR SURE WHAT, IF ANYTHING, THE SUPREME COURT COULD OR SHOULD DO.

THE DEFENDANT:

GEORGIA!

ATLANTA

BACKGROUND: IN 1791 A SOUTH CAROLINA MERCHANT NAMED ROBERT FARQUAR DIED, LEAVING A CONSIDERABLE ESTATE.

WHILE GOING OVER THE DEAD MAN'S PAPERS, CHISHOLM DISCOVERED THAT THE STATE OF GEORGIA OWED THE LATE MR. FARQUAR OODLES OF MONEY FOR GOODS AND SERVICES RENDERED DURING THE REVOLUTIONARY WAR.

FOR THE SAKE OF FARQUAR'S WIDOW AND CHILDREN (NOT TO MENTION HIS FEE), CHISHOLM TRIED TO COLLECT.

$

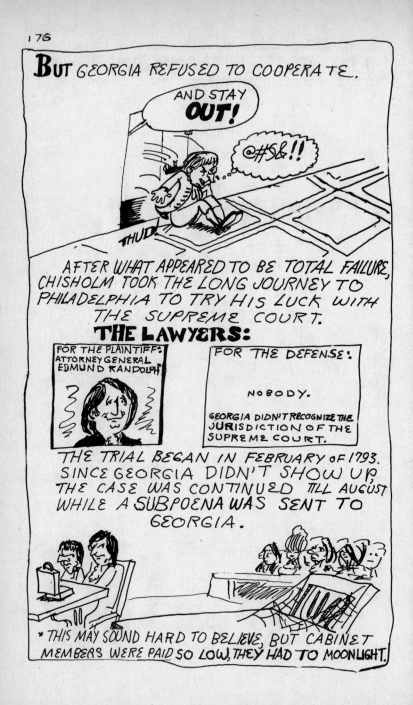

BUT GEORGIA REFUSED TO COOPERATE.

AND STAY **OUT!**

@#$&!!

THUD

AFTER WHAT APPEARED TO BE TOTAL FAILURE, CHISHOLM TOOK THE LONG JOURNEY TO PHILADELPHIA TO TRY HIS LUCK WITH THE SUPREME COURT.

THE LAWYERS:

FOR THE PLAINTIFF: ATTORNEY GENERAL EDMUND RANDOLPH!

FOR THE DEFENSE:

NOBODY.

GEORGIA DIDN'T RECOGNIZE THE JURISDICTION OF THE SUPREME COURT.

THE TRIAL BEGAN IN FEBRUARY OF 1793. SINCE GEORGIA DIDN'T SHOW UP, THE CASE WAS CONTINUED TILL AUGUST WHILE A SUBPOENA WAS SENT TO GEORGIA.

* THIS MAY SOUND HARD TO BELIEVE, BUT CABINET MEMBERS WERE PAID SO LOW, THEY HAD TO MOONLIGHT.

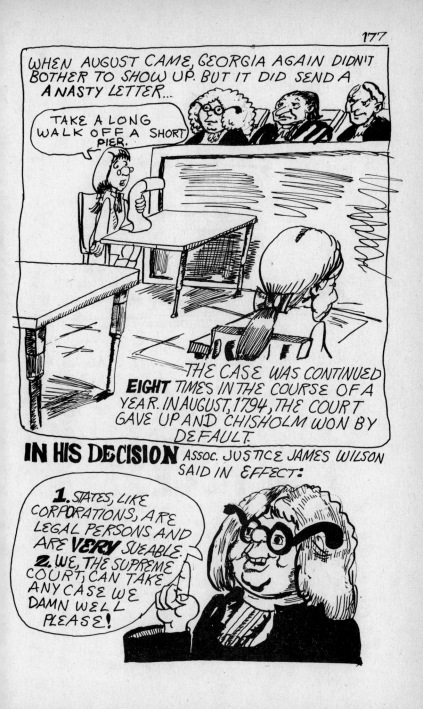

NEEDLESS TO SAY, THE GEORGIA
LEGISLATURE WASN'T VERY HAPPY
ABOUT THE DECISION.

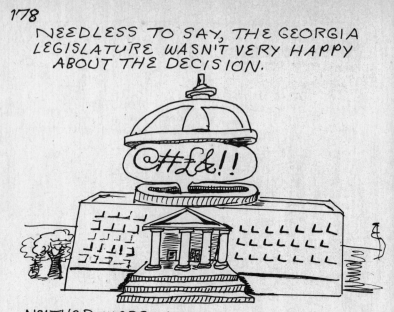

NEITHER WERE NEW YORK, CONNECTICUT
OR MASSACHUSETTS, WHO WERE ALSO BEING
SUED. THE LEGAL EXPERTS WERE
UNANIMOUS — THE ONLY WAY TO OVERTURN
THIS DECISION WAS VIA A CONSTITUTIONAL
AMENDMENT. LOBBYISTS WERE SENT
TO PHILADELPHIA AND IN 1795
CONGRESS PASSED...

ARTICLE XI

The judicial power of the United States shall not be construed to
extend to any suit in law or equity, commenced or prosecuted
against one of the United States by citizens of another State, or by
citizens or subjects of any foreign State.

(THIS TOOK FOUR YEARS TO RATIFY, BY THE WAY.)
THIS THING MEANS THAT IF YOU WANT TO
SUE A STATE, YOU HAVE TO USE STATE
COURTS. BUT NOT IN ALL CASES. IN FACT,
NOT IN MOST! YOU CAN APPEAL STATE COURT JUDG-
MENTS, SUE STATE OFFICIALS AND... THERE ARE MORE
LOOPHOLES HERE THAN IN SWISS CHEESE.

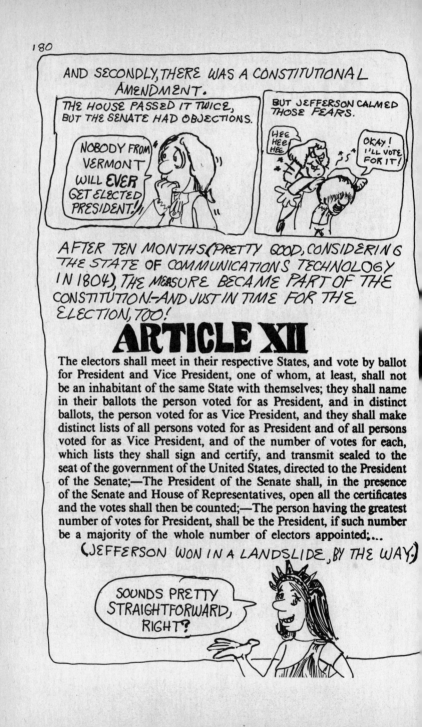

AND SECONDLY, THERE WAS A CONSTITUTIONAL AMENDMENT.

THE HOUSE PASSED IT TWICE, BUT THE SENATE HAD OBJECTIONS.

NOBODY FROM VERMONT WILL **EVER** GET ELECTED PRESIDENT!

BUT JEFFERSON CALMED THOSE FEARS.

HEE HEE HEE

OKAY! I'LL VOTE FOR IT!

AFTER TEN MONTHS (PRETTY GOOD, CONSIDERING THE STATE OF COMMUNICATIONS TECHNOLOGY IN 1804), THE MEASURE BECAME PART OF THE CONSTITUTION—AND JUST IN TIME FOR THE ELECTION, TOO!

ARTICLE XII

The electors shall meet in their respective States, and vote by ballot for President and Vice President, one of whom, at least, shall not be an inhabitant of the same State with themselves; they shall name in their ballots the person voted for as President, and in distinct ballots, the person voted for as Vice President, and they shall make distinct lists of all persons voted for as President and of all persons voted for as Vice President, and of the number of votes for each, which lists they shall sign and certify, and transmit sealed to the seat of the government of the United States, directed to the President of the Senate;—The President of the Senate shall, in the presence of the Senate and House of Representatives, open all the certificates and the votes shall then be counted;—The person having the greatest number of votes for President, shall be the President, if such number be a majority of the whole number of electors appointed;...

(JEFFERSON WON IN A LANDSLIDE, BY THE WAY.)

SOUNDS PRETTY STRAIGHTFORWARD, RIGHT?

HAYES AND WHEELER WERE FORMALLY DECLARED ELECTED ON MARCH 1, 1877.

HAYES WENT ON TO BECOME OUR NATIONS MOST MEDIOCRE PRESIDENT.

NOWADAYS, STATE GOVERNMENTS DETERMINE WHICH PRESIDENTIAL ELECTORS ARE ELECTED.

and if no person have such majority, then from the persons having **the** highest numbers not exceeding three on the list of those voted **for** as President, the House of Representatives shall choose immediately, by the ballot, the President. But in choosing the President, the votes shall be taken by States, the representation from each State having one vote; a quorum for this purpose shall consist of a member or members from two thirds of the States, and a majority of all the States shall be necessary to a choice. And if the House of Representatives shall not choose a President whenever the right of choice shall devolve upon them, before the fourth day of March next following, then the Vice President shall act as President, as in the case of the death or other constitutional disability of the President.

THAT ACTUALLY HAPPENED ONCE!

OF ALL PRESIDENTIAL CAMPAIGNS, THAT OF 1824 RATES AS ONE OF THE THREE OR FOUR WORST. IT LASTED **FIVE** YEARS AND HAD FIVE MAJOR CANDIDATES, ALL OF WHOM WERE **BORING.**

EVEN GENERAL ANDREW JACKSON, WHO HAD CHARISMA COMING OUT OF HIS ARMPITS, WAS A BORE!

GRR

WAKE UP!

THE VOTING WAS VERY LIGHT THAT YEAR BECAUSE EVERYONE WAS SO BORED.

NOBODY WON THAT YEAR, AS YOU CAN SEE BY THE RESULTS:

	POPULAR	ELECTORAL	
JACKSON–J.C. CALHOUN	152,901	99	131 NEEDED TO WIN
J.Q. ADAMS–J.C. CALHOUN	114,023	84	
Wm. CRAWFORD–CALHOUN	46,929	41	
HENRY CLAY–(SOMEONE ELSE.)	47,217	37	

(JOHN C. CALHOUN WAS ELECTED VICE-PRESIDENT IN A LANDSLIDE, BY THE WAY)

HENRY CLAY WAS ELIMINATED.

SO HE MADE A DEAL WITH ADAMS.

LOOK, QUINCE, I FIGURE IT THIS WAY: THE SECOND BEST JOB IN THE COUNTRY IS SECRETARY OF STATE. SO I'LL TRADE YOU MY ELECTORAL VOTES FOR IT.

SOUNDS REASONABLE.

BUT THAT WASN'T QUITE ENOUGH, SO CLAY WENT TO WORK ON THE JACKSON STATES.

MARYLAND VOTES FOR ADAMS.

THIS WAS THE FINAL RESULT:

ADAMS	13
JACKSON	7
CRAWFORD	4

12 NEEDED TO WIN

JOHN QUINCY ADAMS WAS THUS ELECTED OUR SIXTH PRESIDENT.

The person having the greatest number of votes as Vice President shall be the Vice President, if such number be a majority of the whole number of electors appointed, and if no person have a majority, then from the two highest numbers on the list, the Senate shall choose the Vice President; a quorum for the purpose shall consist of two thirds of the whole number of Senators, and a majority of the whole number shall be necessary to a choice. But no person constitutionally ineligible to the office of President shall be eligible to that of Vice President of the United States.

THIS ALSO HAPPENED ONCE.

IN 1836, THE VIRGINIA ELECTORS REFUSED TO VOTE FOR RICHARD M. JOHNSON BECAUSE HE WASN'T A RACIST, LEAVING HIM 12 VOTES SHORT.

THE SENATE ELECTED JOHNSON VICE-PRESIDENT ON A STRICT PARTY LINE VOTE: 33–16.

THINK ABOUT IT.

DICK

THE CIVIL WAR AMENDMENTS (13, 14, 15)

THE CASE OF DRED SCOTT V. EMERSON (XV MO. ST CT 577) SPENT SIX YEARS IN THE COURTS BEFORE THE MISSOURI SUPREME COURT FINALLY GOT TO IT (OR VICE VERSA).

189

DRED SCOTT WAS FREE IN ILLINOIS, BUT IN MISSOURI, HE'S A SLAVE AGAIN.

WHAT'DA WE DO NOW, MISSA HENRY?

TRY AGAIN.

SO SCOTT WAS SOLD TO MRS. EMERSON'S BROTHER JOHN F.A. SANFORD OF NEW YORK AND THE CASE BEGAN ANEW AS **DRED SCOTT v. SANDFORD** (SIC) (1857, 9 HOWARD 33)

IN 1848, THE FEDS STOLE HALF OF MEXICO. THE QUESTION OF SLAVERY IN THE TERRITORIES TOOK ON A NEW IMPORTANCE.

STOLEN 1848

THE SOUTH WANTED THE NEW TERRITORY OPEN TO SLAVERY. THE NORTH DIDN'T.

HENRY CLAY PROPOSED ONE OF HIS FAMOUS COMPROMISES.

CALIFORNIA WILL BE FREE, AND THE REST CAN DECIDE FOR THEMSELVES.

PLUS A TOUGH FUGITIVE SLAVE LAW.

PRES. ZACHARY TAYLOR, WHO WAS AGAINST ANY EXTENSION OF SLAVERY, GAVE HIS OPINION:

THIS @#&!! COMPROMISE WILL PASS ONLY OVER MY DEAD BODY!

AND IT WAS. TAYLOR DIED IN JULY, 1850.

THE PEACE ENVISIONED BY THE COMPROMISE OF 1850 LASTED ONLY A YEAR OR SO. KANSAS WAS IN A STATE OF CIVIL WAR. THE "UNDERGROUND RAILROAD" WAS WORKING OVERTIME.

THE COUNTRY WAS LITERALLY FALLING APART, AND THINGS WERE GETTING WORSE DAY BY DAY...

EVERYBODY KNEW THAT THE SUPREME COURT HAD TO MAKE A PRONOUNCEMENT ON SLAVERY IN THE TERRITORIES. THE DRED SCOTT CASE WAS THE PERFECT VEHICLE FOR IT.

HAVING BEEN TIPPED OFF IN ADVANCE TO THE DECISION, PRES. JAMES BUCHANAN ALLUDED TO IT IN HIS INAUGURAL ADDRESS.

LET US HAPPILY SUBMIT TO THE SUPREME COURT'S DECISION.

HEE! HEE! HEE!

WHICH WENT LIKE THIS (IT WAS READ BY CHIEF JUSTICE ROGER TANEY):

DRED SCOTT IS A SLAVE. NO BLACK, FREE OR OTHERWISE, CAN BE A CITIZEN.

BECAUSE BLACKS ARE PROPERTY AND NOT PEOPLE, THE LAW MAKING WISCONSON A FREE TERRITORY IS UNCONSTITUTIONAL, VIOLATING THE FIFTH AMENDMENT'S DUE PROCESS CLAUSE PROTECTING PROPERTY.

DRED SCOTT WAS STILL A SLAVE. HENRY BLOW AND JOHN SANFORD FREED HIM A COUPLE OF DAYS LATER...

THINGS GOT WORSE. TANEY WAS BURNED IN EFFIGY. JOHN BROWN'S RAID TOOK PLACE LESS THAN TWO YEAR LATER.

THEN, IN 1860...

AN ABOLITIONIST* NAMED ABRAHAM LINCOLN WAS ELECTED PRESIDENT WITH ONLY 39% OF THE POPULAR VOTE.

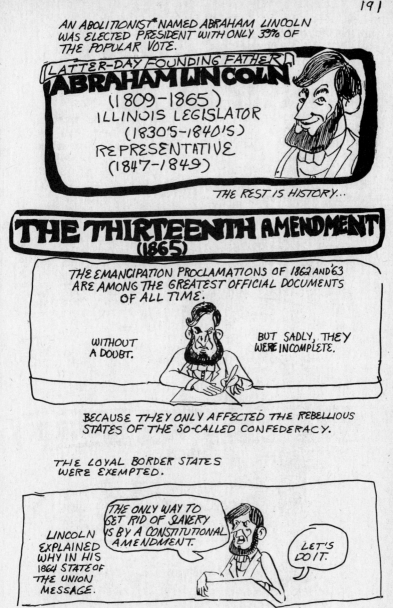

LATTER-DAY FOUNDING FATHER

ABRAHAM LINCOLN

(1809-1865)
ILLINOIS LEGISLATOR
(1830'S-1840'S)
REPRESENTATIVE
(1847-1849)

THE REST IS HISTORY...

THE THIRTEENTH AMENDMENT
(1865)

THE EMANCIPATION PROCLAMATIONS OF 1862 AND '63 ARE AMONG THE GREATEST OFFICIAL DOCUMENTS OF ALL TIME.

WITHOUT A DOUBT.

BUT SADLY, THEY WERE INCOMPLETE.

BECAUSE THEY ONLY AFFECTED THE REBELLIOUS STATES OF THE SO-CALLED CONFEDERACY.

THE LOYAL BORDER STATES WERE EXEMPTED.

LINCOLN EXPLAINED WHY IN HIS 1864 STATE OF THE UNION MESSAGE.

THE ONLY WAY TO GET RID OF SLAVERY IS BY A CONSTITUTIONAL AMENDMENT.

LET'S DO IT.

*A PERSON WHO WANTS THE ABOLITION OF SLAVERY.

IT FAILED IN THE HOUSE THREE TIMES IN 1864 (THE
SENATE PASSED IT IMMEDIATELY) BEFORE IT WAS
SENT TO THE STATES IN JANUARY, 1865. IT GOT THE
REQUISITE THREE-FOURTHS IN DECEMBER.

ARTICLE XIII

Section 1. Neither slavery nor involuntary servitude, except as punishment for crime whereof the party shall have been duly convicted, shall exist within the United States, or any place subject to their jurisdiction.

Section 2. Congress shall have power to enforce this article by appropriate legislation.

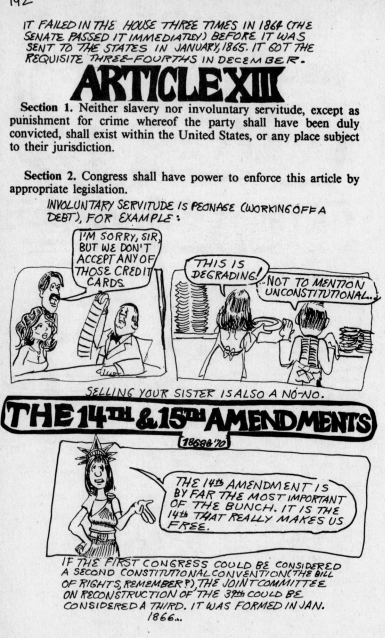

INVOLUNTARY SERVITUDE IS PEONAGE (WORKING OFF A DEBT), FOR EXAMPLE:

I'M SORRY, SIR, BUT WE DON'T ACCEPT ANY OF THOSE CREDIT CARDS.

THIS IS DEGRADING!

NOT TO MENTION UNCONSTITUTIONAL...

SELLING YOUR SISTER IS ALSO A NO-NO.

THE 14TH & 15TH AMENDMENTS
(1868 & '70)

THE 14th AMENDMENT IS BY FAR THE MOST IMPORTANT OF THE BUNCH. IT IS THE 14th THAT REALLY MAKES US FREE.

IF THE FIRST CONGRESS COULD BE CONSIDERED A SECOND CONSTITUTIONAL CONVENTION (THE BILL OF RIGHTS, REMEMBER?), THE JOINT COMMITTEE ON RECONSTRUCTION OF THE 39th COULD BE CONSIDERED A THIRD. IT WAS FORMED IN JAN. 1866...

1866 WAS A VERY WEIRD YEAR. UNDER THE ULTRA-LENIENT ANDREW JOHNSON RECONSTRUCTION PROGRAM, THE FORMER CONFEDERACY BEGAN A PROGRAM OF RE-ENSLAVEMENT OF AFRO-AMERICANS CALLED "BLACK CODES."

IT WAS THE JOB OF THE JOINT COMMITTEE TO PUT AN END TO THIS PRACTICE AND TO BEGIN REBUILDING A NATION TRULY BASED ON OUR FOUNDING PRINCIPLES...

...LIFE, LIBERTY, EQUALITY... THAT SORT OF THING.

IN ORDER TO, IN EFFECT, WRITE A NEW CONSTITUTION TO FIT THE TIMES, WE NEED A NEW JAMES MADISON.

AND WE JUST HAPPENED TO HAVE ONE LYING AROUND...

LATTER-DAY FOUNDING FATHER
JOHN A. BINGHAM
(1815-1900)
REPRESENTATIVE
(1855-'63, 1865-'73)

BINGHAM SAW A NUMBER OF PROBLEMS THAT NEEDED CORRECTION...

THE FIRST THING WE HAVE TO CHANGE IS THE DRED SCOTT DECISION. IT'S OBSCENE, BUT TOTALLY CORRECT, LEGALLY, THAT IS... SO WE NEED A DEFINITION OF WHO'S A CITIZEN.

SECOND: ART. 4 §2 HAS TO GO. SINCE CORFIELD v. CORYELL AND BARRON v. BALTIMORE IT HAS BEEN A TOTAL JOKE. SO WE CHANGE IT, MAKING THE BILL OF RIGHTS EFFECTIVE ON THE STATES.

AND, OH YEAH, A NEW IMPROVED CENSUS WOULD BE NICE!

SNAP

WHILE BINGHAM AND THE OTHER MEMBERS OF THE COMMITTEE WERE WORKING ON THE AMENDMENTS, CONGRESS PASSED THE CIVIL RIGHTS ACT OF 1866. PRES. JOHNSON VETOED IT BECAUSE IT WAS...

UNCONSTITUTIONAL!

WHICH IS WHY WE NEEDED A CONSTITUTIONAL AMENDMENT IN THE FIRST PLACE.

CONGRESS OVERRODE THE VETO, BY THE WAY.

CONGRESS REFUSED TO RE-ADMIT THE FORMER CONFEDERATE STATES UNLESS THEY RATIFIED THE 14th AMENDMENT (WHICH BARELY PASSED CONGRESS IN JUNE, 1866). WHILE MOST DID, SOME DIDN'T AND SOME NORTHERN STATES WHICH HAD RATIFIED QUICKLY TRIED TO DE-RATIFY, BUT IT DIDN'T WORK.

IT BECAME PART OF THE CONSTITUTION ON JULY 28, 1868.

ARTICLE XIV

FOR REASONS THAT WILL BECOME APPARENT LATER, WE WILL START WITH §3.

Section 3. No person shall be a senator or representative in Congress, or elector of President and Vice President, or hold any office, civil or military, under the United States, or under any State, who having previously taken an oath, as a member of Congress, or as an officer of the United States, or as a member of any State legislature, or as an executive or judicial officer of any State, to support the Constitution of the United States, shall have engaged in insurrection or rebellion against the same, or given aid or comfort to the enemies thereof. But Congress may by a vote of two-thirds of each House, remove such disability.

THIS WAS PUT HERE IN ORDER TO PUNISH THE CONFEDERATES FOR HAVING THE GALL TO GO TO WAR FOR A CAUSE AS VILE AS SLAVERY. IT WAS REPEALED, AS THE LAST SENTENCE SPECIFIED, IN 1898. BUT MOST EX-REBELS HAD BEEN RE-ENFRANCHISED LONG BEFORE.

Section 4. The validity of the public debt of the United States, authorized by law, including debts incurred for payment of pensions and bounties for services in suppressing insurrection or rebellion, shall not be questioned. But neither the United States nor any State shall assume or pay any debt or obligation incurred in aid of insurrection or rebellion against the United States, or any claim for the loss or emancipation of any slave; but all such debts, obligations, and claims shall be held illegal and void.

Section 5. The Congress shall have power to enforce, by appropriate legislation, the provisions of this article.

CIVIL RIGHTS CASES (1883, 109 US.3) (SIX OF 'EM.)

§1: THE HEAVY STUFF

All persons born or naturalized in the United States, and subject to the jurisdiction thereof, are citizens of the United States and of the State wherein they reside.

IF IT HADN'T BEEN FOR THE DRED SCOTT DECISION, BINGHAM AND HIS COMPATRIOTS WOULDN'T HAVE EVEN BOTHERED.

BUT THERE'S ONE THING THAT MUST BE REMEMBERED: EVERYTHING IN §1 HAD TO BE FOUGHT FOR AFTER RATIFICATION

SOMETIMES SEVERAL TIMES.

EVEN THAT SENTENCE, UP THERE!

THE CASE: U.S. v. WONG KIM ARK
(1898, 169 US 649)

SAN FRANCISCO, 1890

AHH! ITS GOOD TO BE HOME!

EXCUSE ME, MAC.

BUT CHINKS AREN'T ALLOWED IN THE UNITED STATES.

THAT'S OKAY

I'M AN ASIAN-AMERICAN, BORN RIGHT HERE IN SAN FRANSISCO

ASIAN SCHMASIAN, YOU'RE STILL A CHINK AND CHINKS AIN'T ALLOWED IN THE U.S.A!

I'M A NATURAL-BORN CITIZEN, DAMMIT!

NO, YOU'RE NOT!

WONG GOT A WRIT OF HABEAS CORPUS THREE DAYS LATER...

AFTER SEVEN YEARS OF UNEXPLAINABLE LITIGATION, THE CASE GOT TO THE SUPREME COURT.

ASSOC. JUSTICE HORACE GRAY OPINED:

IT'S AS CLEAR AS A BELL: ANYBODY, EXCEPT THE CHILDREN OF FOREIGN DIPLOMATS, BORN IN THE U.S.A. IS A CITIZEN.

NEVER UNDERESTIMATE THE POWER OF RACISM —EVER!

THIS, TO SOME, IS THE MOST IMPORTANT CLAUSE IN THE WHOLE CONSTITUTION.

IF IT LOOKS FAMILIAR, IT'S BECAUSE IT WAS LIFTED ALMOST INTACT FROM ART. 4 §2 AND GIVEN SOME IMPROVEMENT.

No State shall make or enforce any law which shall abridge the privileges or immunities of citizens of the United States;

AND TO BE ABSOLUTELY SURE THE STATES WOULDN'T, BINGHAM RESTATED PART OF THE 5th AMENDMENT:

nor shall any State deprive any person of life, liberty, or property, without due process of law;

ALL WELL AND GOOD. UNTIL SOMEBODY TRIED, THAT IS.

THE SLAUGHTERHOUSE CASES

(1873, 18 WALLACE 36)

IN 1869, THE STATE OF LOUISIANA SET UP A COMPANY CALLED THE CRESCENT CITY LIVESTOCK AND SLAUGHTER HOUSE CO. AND GAVE IT A MONOPOLY IN THE NEW ORLEANS METRO AREA. AS A RESULT, ALMOST ALL THAT CITY'S BUTCHERS LOST THEIR BUSINESSES.

THE 14th AMENDMENT WAS PASSED TO PROTECT **BLACKS.** THE VICTIMS HERE ARE **WHITE!** IT THEREFORE DOESN'T WORK.

ASSOC. JUSTICE STEPHEN FIELD MADE A STIRRING DISSENT:

IN UPHOLDING THE VIRTUAL THEFT OF MILLIONS OF DOLLARS IN BUSINESS, ASSOC. JUSTICE SAMUEL MILLER SAID IN EFFECT (IT WAS A 5-4 DECISION):

THE 14th AMENDMENT DOESN'T CREATE ANY NEW RIGHTS AND PRIVILEGES OR IMMUNITIES, BUT IT MAKES THEM EFFECTIVE ON THE STATES.

BESIDES, IT DOESN'T MENTION RACE ANYWHERE, SO IT PROTECTS ANYBODY.

THIS, PLUS THE CIVIL RIGHTS CASES DECISION GUTTED THE 14th AMENDMENT. IT WAS OFFICIALLY IGNORED BY THE SUPREME COURT FOR 50 YEARS.

GITLOW v. N.Y. (1925)

(268 U S 652)

BEN GITLOW WAS A COMMIE.

HE RAN A PAPER CALLED THE "REVOLUTIONARY AGE."

IN 1919 HE WROTE AN INCREDIBLY BORING ARTICLE CALLED "THE LEFT WING MANIFESTO."

HE WAS ARRESTED AND CHARGED WITH SEDITION UNDER THE NEW YORK ANTI-SEDITION LAW.

GITLOW WAS CONVICTED AND HIS EVERY APPEAL FAILED. (HE WAS LATER PARDONED BY GOV. AL SMITH, AND THE PUBLICITY CAUSED BY THE CASE GOT HIM THE 1928 COMMUNIST NOMINATION FOR VICE-PRESIDENT.)

IF ALL THE APPEALS FAILED, WHAT GOOD IS IT AS A PRECEDENT?

THE ANSWER IS IN ASSOC. JUSTICE EDWARD T. SANFORD'S OPINION:

FOR THE PRESENT PURPOSES, WE MAY AND DO ASSUME THAT FREEDOM OF SPEECH AND THE PRESS, WHICH ARE PROTECTED BY THE FIRST AMENDMENT FROM ABRIDGMENT BY CONGRESS, ARE AMONG THE FUNDAMENTAL RIGHTS AND LIBERTIES PROTECTED BY THE DUE PROCESS CLAUSE OF THE 14th AMENDMENT FROM IMPAIRMENT BY THE STATES, HOWEVER...

HUH?

IT IS THIS ASSUMPTION WHICH IS THE BASIS OF AMERICAN FREEDOM, AND HENCE ITS GREATNESS.

THE 14th AMENDMENT'S INCORPORATION
OF THE BILL OF RIGHTS HAS BEEN A LONG
AND VERY PAINFUL PROCESS, BUT BY 1983,
WHEN THE 3rd AMENDMENT WAS INCORPORATED
(ENGELBLOOM v. CAREY, 1983, 667 F.2nd 957), PROBABLY
ALL OF IT THAT EVER WAS GOING TO BE
INCORPORATED HAS BEEN.

THE SECOND, SEVENTH
AND TENTH AMENDMENTS,
BY THEIR CONSTRUCTION,
CANNOT BE INCORPORATED

AND SOME STATES
HAVE FOUND FAIRER
AND MORE EFFECTIVE
SYSTEMS OF INDICTING
PEOPLE THAN BY
GRAND JURY

nor deny to any person
within its jurisdiction
the equal protection of
the laws.

THIS MEANS THAT DISCRIMINATION ON ACCOUNT
OF RACE, RELIGION. OR SOMETIMES SEX IS VERBOTEN!

THE RIGHT TO VOTE

THE RIGHT TO VOTE WAS FIRST RECOGNIZED
IN THE NEW, IMPROVED CENSUS CREATED IN
THE 14th AMENDMENT...

Section 2. Representatives shall be apportioned among the several
States according to their respective numbers, counting the whole
number of persons in each State, excluding Indians not taxed. But
when the right to vote at any election for the choice of electors for
President and Vice President of the United States, representatives
in Congress, the executive and judicial officers of a State, or the
members of the legislature thereof, is denied to any of the male
inhabitants of such State, being twenty-one years of age, and citizens
of the United States, or in any way abridged, except for participation
in rebellion, or other crime, the basis of representation therein shall
be reduced in the proportion which the number of such male citizens
shall bear to the whole number of male citizens twenty-one years
of age in such State.

IN 1870, AN APPENDIX WAS ADDED.

ARTICLE XV

Section 1. The right of citizens of the United States to vote shall not be denied or abridged by the United States or by any State on account of race, color, or previous condition of servitude.

Section 2. The Congress shall have power to enforce this article by appropriate legislation.

IT IS VERY RARE, INDEED, WHEN THE SUPREME COURT CALLS THE CONSTITUTION A LIAR,

BUT

IN 1874, AN ELECTION OFFICIAL NAMED REECE REFUSED TO LET REGISTERED BLACK VOTERS VOTE. THE FEDS SUED...

THE OPINION IN U.S. v. REESE (1875, 92 US 52) IS A (TWISTED) WONDER TO BEHOLD.

THERE IS NO RIGHT TO VOTE. SINCE IT DOESN'T EXIST IN THE FIRST PLACE, IT CAN'T BE DENIED OR ABRIDGED.

ELECTION OFFICIALS CAN DO WHATEVER THEY WANT.

NINE YEARS LATER, IN A THEN RARE ATTACK OF SANITY, THE COURT REVERSED ITSELF IN EX PARTE YARBROUGH (110 U.S. 651)

MAYBE VOTING IS A RIGHT?

BUT THIS WAS ONLY A TEMPORARY VICTORY. IN THE 1890'S AND EARLY 1900'S THE COURTS AND CONGRESS TOTALLY ABANDONED BLACKS. RACISTS PASSED ALL SORTS OF DISCRIMINATORY VOTING LAWS.

LIKE "GRANDFATHER CLAUSES."

ANYBODY WHOSE GRANDFATHER WAS A NATURAL-BORN AMERICAN, BUT NOT A CITIZEN IN 1867, IS DISENFRANCHISED FOREVER.

THE SIXTEENTH AMENDMENT: THE INCOME TAX! (1913)

THE INCOME TAX WAS INVENTED BY PRES. LINCOLN IN ORDER TO PAY FOR THE CIVIL WAR.

FREEDOM AIN'T CHEAP.

WHEN THE WAR ENDED, SO DID THE TAX. IN 1894 CONGRESS CREATED A NEW ONE. TWO YEARS LATER, THE SUPREME COURT DECLARED IT UNCONSTITUTIONAL.

THE INCOME TAX BECAME A MAJOR LIBERAL ISSUE.

SOAK THE RICH!

BUT THE LIBERALS DIDN'T GET IT PASSED!

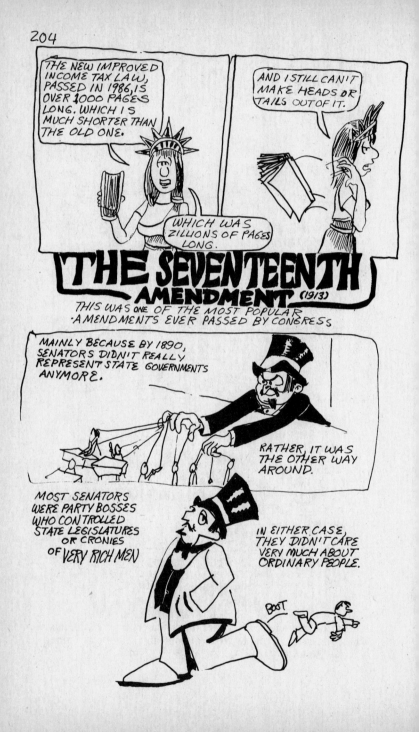

THE NEW IMPROVED INCOME TAX LAW, PASSED IN 1986, IS OVER 1000 PAGES LONG. WHICH IS MUCH SHORTER THAN THE OLD ONE.

AND I STILL CAN'T MAKE HEADS OR TAILS OUT OF IT.

WHICH WAS ZILLIONS OF PAGES LONG.

THE SEVENTEENTH AMENDMENT (1913)

THIS WAS ONE OF THE MOST POPULAR AMENDMENTS EVER PASSED BY CONGRESS

MAINLY BECAUSE BY 1890, SENATORS DIDN'T REALLY REPRESENT STATE GOVERNMENTS ANYMORE.

RATHER, IT WAS THE OTHER WAY AROUND.

MOST SENATORS WERE PARTY BOSSES WHO CONTROLLED STATE LEGISLATURES OR CRONIES OF VERY RICH MEN

IN EITHER CASE, THEY DIDN'T CARE VERY MUCH ABOUT ORDINARY PEOPLE.

BOOT

POPULAR ELECTION OF SENATORS WASN'T NEW.
THE IDEA HAD BEEN POPPING UP SINCE THE 1830's.
BUT THE MOVEMENT HAD BEGUN IN ERNEST
IN 1893, WHEN THE HOUSE PASSED THE
PROPOSED AMENDMENT FOR THE FIRST
TIME. THE SENATE IGNORED IT, AS IT DID THE
NEXT EIGHT TIMES AS WELL.

SO A DIFFERENT
TACK WAS USED...

FOR THE FIRST TIME
STATE LEGISLATURES BEGAN
PETITIONING CONGRESS FOR
A SECOND CONSTITUTIONAL
CONVENTION IN AN ORGANIZED
FASHION.

IN 1911
ENOUGH STATES
HAD PETITIONED
CONGRESS TO
FORCE A
CONVENTION.

HOLD IT!

VOTE FOR ME

...AND NOT ONLY THAT,
SEN. WILLIAM LOREMER
WAS CAUGHT BRIBING
STATE LEGISLATORS TO
GET RE-ELECTED.

FACED WITH A DANGEROUS CONVENTION AND A
MAJOR SCANDAL, THE SENATE FINALLY PASSED
WHAT WOULD BECOME...

ARTICLE XVII

The Senate of the United States shall be composed of two senators
from each state, elected by the people thereof, for six years; and
each senator shall have one vote. The electors in each State shall
have the qualifications requisite for electors of the most numerous
branch of the State legislature.

SENATORS NOW
REPRESENT PEOPLE,
NOT REAL ESTATE.

A BIG
IMPROVEMENT!

When vacancies happen in the representation of any State in the Senate, the executive authority of such State shall issue writs of election to fill such vacancies: *Provided,* That the legislature of any State may empower the executive thereof to make temporary appointments until the people fill the vacancies by election as the legislature may direct.

IN 1976 MINNESOTA GOV. WENDELL ANDERSON MADE HIMSELF A SENATOR.

IN THE 1978 SPECIAL ELECTION HE GOT CREAMED. MOST OTHER GOVERNORS APPOINT FRIENDS TO SENATE VACANCIES. IT'S SAFER.

This amendment shall not be so construed as to affect the election or term of any senator chosen before it becomes valid as part of the Constitution. IN OTHER WORDS, NOBODY GETS FIRED.

PROHIBITION: AMENDMENTS 18 & 21

IT'S ALWAYS A MISTAKE TO LEGISLATE MORALITY.

ESPECIALLY WHEN A HUGE AMOUNT OF PEOPLE ARE IMMORAL.

GRANTED THERE **WAS** A PROBLEM. PARTLY DUE TO ABYSMAL WORKING CONDITIONS ALCOHOLISM WAS ENDEMIC.

FATHER DEAR FATHER COME HOME WITH ME NOW

ETC ETC ETC

IT WAS COMMON FOR WORKING MEN TO DRINK UP THEIR SALARIES AND THEN GO HOME AND BEAT UP THEIR WIVES. SOMETHING HAD TO BE DONE.

IN 1872 THE PROHIBITION PARTY "WAS
FORMED TO LEAD THE FIGHT TO BAN BOOZE.
THE LATER, NON-PARTISAN, "ANTI-SALOON
LEAGUE" WAS FORMED IN 1895. IT SOON
BECAME THE FIRST HIGH-POWERED
SPECIAL INTEREST LOBBY AND WAS HIGHLY
SUCCESSFUL. BY 1916, 14 STATES HAD
BANNED BOOZE. IN DECEMBER, 1917,
ALMOST BY ACCIDENT CONGRESS PASSED
A PROPOSED AMENDMENT. IT WAS
RATIFIED IN 1919.

ARTICLE XVIII (1919)

After one year from the ratification of this article, the manufacture, sale, or transportation of intoxicating liquors within, the importation thereof into, or the exportation thereof from the United States and all territory subject to the jurisdiction thereof for beverage purposes is hereby prohibited.

The Congress and the several States shall have concurrent power to enforce this article by appropriate legislation.

This article shall be inoperative unless it shall have been ratified as an amendment to the Constitution by the legislatures of the several States, as provided in the Constitution, within seven years from the date of the submission hereof to the states by Congress.

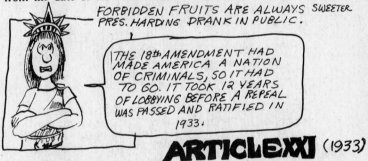

FORBIDDEN FRUITS ARE ALWAYS SWEETER.
PRES. HARDING DRANK IN PUBLIC.

THE 18th AMENDMENT HAD
MADE AMERICA A NATION
OF CRIMINALS, SO IT HAD
TO GO. IT TOOK 12 YEARS
OF LOBBYING BEFORE A REPEAL
WAS PASSED AND RATIFIED IN
1933.

ARTICLE XXI (1933)

Section 1. The Eighteenth Article of amendment to the Constitution of the United States is hereby repealed. DRINKING IS LEGAL! WOOPEE!

Section 2. The transporation or importation into any State, Territory, or possession of the United States for delivery or use therein of intoxicating liquors in violation of the laws thereof, is hereby prohibited.

STATES CAN NOW, IF THEY WISH, BAN THE
IMPORTATION OF BOOZE, BUT THEY NEVER
ACTUALLY HAVE. (SUCCESSFULLY, THAT IS.)

Section 3. This article shall be inoperative unless it shall have been ratified as an amendment to the Constitution by conventions in the several States, as provided in the Constitution, within seven years from the date of the submission thereof to the States by the Congress.

RATIFICATION BY CONVENTIONS IS A NATIONAL PLEBICITE BASED ON THE ELECTORAL COLLEGE SYSTEM.

THE PEOPLE (SORT OF), NOT POLITICIANS, RATIFIED THIS ONE. (E.R.A. PEOPLE PLEASE NOTE.)

THE 19TH AMENDMENT (1920)

THE HEROIC STRUGGLE BY WOMEN TO GET THE VOTE SHOULD HAVE BEGUN IN 1780 WHEN MASSACHUSETTS DISENFRANCHISED WOMEN, OR IN 1807, WHEN NEW JERSEY DID THE SAME THING. (WOMEN COULDN'T VOTE ANYWHERE ELSE.) BUT IT DIDN'T. INSTEAD, IT BEGAN IN THE 1848 SENECA FALLS CONVENTION.

THE FIRST SUFFRAGETTES WERE PART OF THE ABOLITION MOVEMENT.

FREEDOM AND EQALITY FOR BLACKS!

HEAR, HEAR.

FREEDOM AND EQUALITY FOR WOMEN!

RIGHT ON.

AFTER THE MEN IN THE ABOLITION MOVEMENT ABANDONED THEIR FEMALE COMPATRIOTS IN 1865, THE LADIES TOOK A DIFFERENT TURN.

MINOR v. HAPPERSETT (1875, 21 WALLACE 162)

HELLO MR. HAPPERSETT I'D LIKE TO REGISTER AND VOTE.

I'M SORRY, MA'AM, BUT YOU CAN'T.

AND WHY NOT?

WHY DO YOU THINK, MADAME?!

BACK TO THE KITCHEN WITH YOU!

AS YOU MIGHT HAVE SUSPECTED, MRS. MINOR SUED HAPPERSETT ON THE GROUNDS THAT HE HAD VIOLATED THE EQUAL PROTECTION CLAUSE OF THE 14th AMENDMENT, PLUS ALL OF ITS §2.

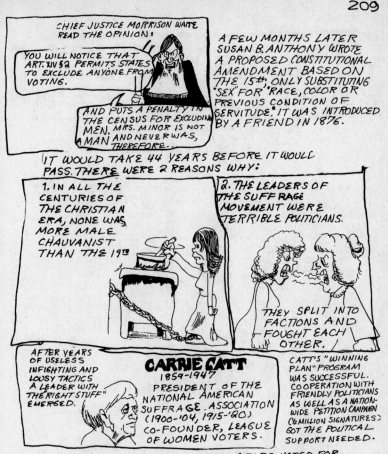

ARTICLE XX

The right of citizens of the United States to vote shall not be denied or abridged by the United States or by any State on account of sex.

The Congress shall have power by appropriate legislation to enforce the provisions of this article.

ARTICLE XX

Section 1. The terms of the President and Vice President shall end at noon on the 20th day of January, and the terms of Senators and Representatives at noon on the 3d day of January, of the years in which such terms would have ended if this article had not been ratified; and the terms of their successors shall then begin.

IN OTHER WORDS, THE PRESIDENT, VICEPRESIDENT AND CONGRESS GOT CHEATED OUT OF THEIR LAST THREE MONTHS IN OFFICE.

Section 2. The Congress shall assemble at least once in every year, and such meeting shall begin at noon on the 3d day of January, unless they shall by law appoint a different day.

NO MORE LAME-DUCK SESSIONS!! NEWLY ELECTED CONGRESS PERSONS WOULDN'T HAVE TO WAIT ELEVEN MONTHS TO TAKE OFFICE.

PLUS, WE INCUMBENTS CAN EXTEND OUR CHRISTMAS VACATIONS IF WE SO WISH!

Section 3. If, at the time fixed for the beginning of the term of the President, the President-elect shall have died, the Vice President-elect shall become President. If a President shall not have been chosen before the time fixed for the beginning of his term, or if the President-elect shall have failed to qualify, then the Vice President-elect shall act as President until a President shall have qualified; and the Congress may by law provide for the case wherein neither a President-elect nor a Vice President-elect shall have qualified, declaring who shall then act as President, or the manner in which one who is to act shall be selected, and such person shall act acccordingly until a President or Vice President shall have qualified.

IT WORKS LIKE THIS:

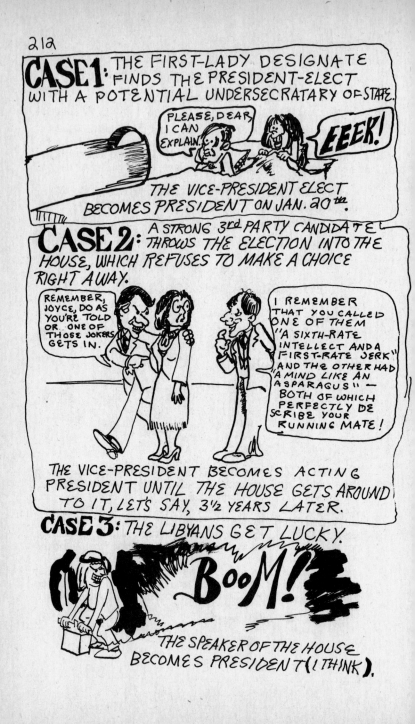

CASE 1: THE FIRST-LADY DESIGNATE FINDS THE PRESIDENT-ELECT WITH A POTENTIAL UNDERSECRETARY OF STATE.

PLEASE, DEAR I CAN EXPLAIN.

EEER!

THE VICE-PRESIDENT ELECT BECOMES PRESIDENT ON JAN. 20th.

CASE 2: A STRONG 3rd PARTY CANDIDATE THROWS THE ELECTION INTO THE HOUSE, WHICH REFUSES TO MAKE A CHOICE RIGHT AWAY.

REMEMBER, JOYCE, DO AS YOU'RE TOLD OR ONE OF THOSE JOKERS GETS IN.

I REMEMBER THAT YOU CALLED ONE OF THEM "A SIXTH-RATE INTELLECT AND A FIRST-RATE JERK" AND THE OTHER HAD "A MIND LIKE AN ASPARAGUS" — BOTH OF WHICH PERFECTLY DESCRIBE YOUR RUNNING MATE!

THE VICE-PRESIDENT BECOMES ACTING PRESIDENT UNTIL THE HOUSE GETS AROUND TO IT, LET'S SAY, 3½ YEARS LATER.

CASE 3: THE LIBYANS GET LUCKY.

BOOM!

THE SPEAKER OF THE HOUSE BECOMES PRESIDENT (I THINK).

Section 4. The Congress may by law provide for the case of the death of any of the persons from whom the House of Representatives may choose a President whenever the right of choice shall have devolved upon them, and for the case of the death of any of the persons from whom the Senate may choose a Vice President whenever the right of choice shall have devolved upon them.

UH... YEAH, WHY NOT?

Section 5. Sections 1 and 2 shall take effect on the 15th day of October following the ratification of this article.

THIS WAS PUT HERE TO GET RID OF HERBERT HOOVER. IT DIDN'T WORK

Section 6. This article shall be inoperative unless it shall have been ratified as an amendment to the Constitution by the legislatures of three-fourths of the several States within seven years from the date of its submission

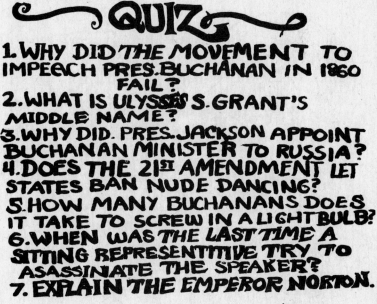

QUIZ

1. WHY DID THE MOVEMENT TO IMPEACH PRES. BUCHANAN IN 1860 FAIL?

2. WHAT IS ULYSSES S. GRANT'S MIDDLE NAME?

3. WHY DID PRES. JACKSON APPOINT BUCHANAN MINISTER TO RUSSIA?

4. DOES THE 21ST AMENDMENT LET STATES BAN NUDE DANCING?

5. HOW MANY BUCHANANS DOES IT TAKE TO SCREW IN A LIGHT BULB?

6. WHEN WAS THE LAST TIME A SITTING REPRESENTITIVE TRY TO ASASSINATE THE SPEAKER?

7. EXPLAIN THE EMPEROR NORTON.

1. BECAUSE STUPIDITY ISN'T AN IMPEACHABLE OFFENSE.
2. HIRAM.
3. BECAUSE THE U.S. HAS NO DIPLOMATIC RELATIONS WITH THE NORTH POLE.
4. YES, THOUGH WE STILL CAN'T FIGURE OUT WHY.
5. NONE. HE DIED BEFORE IT WAS INVENTED.
6. MARCH 4, 1911.
7. TRICK QUESTION; NOBODY CAN EXPLAIN THE EMPEROR NORTON.

THE TWENTY-SECOND AMENDMENT (1951)

THE MAIN REASON FOR THIS ONE WAS SPITE, PURE AND SIMPLE.

BUT IT WASN'T THE ONLY REASON. FOR THE "NO THIRD TERM FOR PRESIDENTS TRADITION" WAS A LONG AND HALLOWED ONE...

THE REPUBLICANS WANTED REVENGE SO BAD THEY COULD TASTE IT ...AND IN 1947, WITH THEIR FIRST MAJORITY IN SEVENTEEN YEARS, THEY HAD THEIR CHANCE...

SJ3 PASSED THE SENATE BY VOICE VOTE, AND THE HOUSE BY 285-121.

"...PUTTIN' ON THE RITZ!"

FRANKLIN DELANO ROOSEVELT 1882-1945

FOUR YEARS LATER, IT BECAME...

ARTICLE XXII

Section 1. No person shall be elected to the office of the President more than twice, and no person who has held the office of President, or acted as President, for more than two years of a term to which some other person was elected President shall be elected to the office of the President more than once. But this article shall not apply to any person holding the office of President when this article was proposed by the Congress, and shall not prevent any person who may be holding the office of President, or acting as President, during the term within which this article becomes operative from holding the office of President or acting as President during the remainder of such term.

Section 2. This article shall be inoperative unless it shall have been ratified as an amendment to the Constitution by the legislatures of three-fourths of the several States within seven years from the date of its submission to the States by the Congress.

IN OTHER WORDS, NOBODY CAN BE PRESIDENT MORE THAN TEN YEARS...

THE TWENTY-THIRD AMENDMENT (1961)

SYNOPSIS: WHEN LAST WE LEFT THE DISTRICT OF COLUMBIA (BACK ON PAGE 104) IT HAD JUST LOST SELF-GOVERNMENT AND WAS BACK UNDER CONGRESSIONAL CONTROL...

D.C. TWO
YOU CAN'T ALWAYS GET WHAT YOU WANT

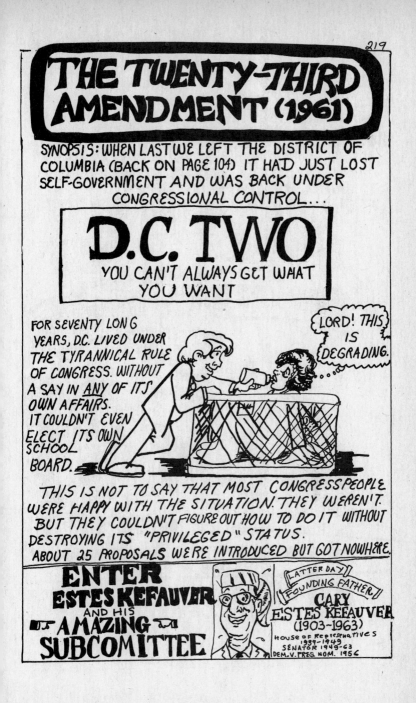

FOR SEVENTY LONG YEARS, D.C. LIVED UNDER THE TYRANNICAL RULE OF CONGRESS. WITHOUT A SAY IN ANY OF ITS OWN AFFAIRS. IT COULDN'T EVEN ELECT ITS OWN SCHOOL BOARD.

LORD! THIS IS DEGRADING...

THIS IS NOT TO SAY THAT MOST CONGRESSPEOPLE WERE HAPPY WITH THE SITUATION. THEY WEREN'T. BUT THEY COULDN'T FIGURE OUT HOW TO DO IT WITHOUT DESTROYING ITS "PRIVILEGED" STATUS. ABOUT 25 PROPOSALS WERE INTRODUCED BUT GOT NOWHERE.

ENTER ESTES KEFAUVER AND HIS AMAZING SUBCOMMITTEE

LATTER DAY FOUNDING FATHER
CARY ESTES KEFAUVER (1903-1963)
HOUSE OF REPRESENTATIVES 1939-1949
SENATOR 1949-63
DEM. V. PRES. NOM. 1956

LADIES & GENTLEMEN!! YOUR ATTENTION, *PLEASE!* SEN. KEFAUVER AND HIS AMAZING SUBCOMMITTEE** WILL ATTEMPT FOR YOUR READING *PLEASURE* TO GET 3 (COUNT 'EM, 3) CONSTITUTIONAL AMENDMENTS PAST THESE *FEROCIOUS SOUTHERN SENATORS* TO MY LEFT!

...AND GET THEM SAFELY INTO THE HOUSE!

THE PACKAGE OF THREE AMENDMENTS (CALLED SJ23) CONTAINED:

1. GIVING GOVERNORS THE POWER TO FILL VACANCIES IN THE HOUSE FOR UP TO 60 DAYS.

2. AN END TO POLL TAXES FOREVER! (SEE OUR NEXT EXITING CHAPTER FOR FURTHER DETAILS)

3. FULL STATEHOOD RIGHTS FOR D.C. (EXCEPT SENATORS). (THIS WAS AUTHORED BY JACOB JAVITS & K. KEATING)

THE HOUSE VACANCY AMENDMENT WAS TOTALLY OBLITERATED, NEVER TO SEE THE LIGHT OF DAY AGAIN. THE OTHER TWO DIDN'T FARE MUCH BETTER...

THE FRAGMENT WAS PASSED BY VOICE VOTE ON JUNE 16, 1960, AND IN 1961 BECAME...

ARTICLE XXIII

Section 1. The district constituting the seat of Government of the United States shall appoint in such manner as the Congress may direct:

A number of electors of President and Vice President equal to the whole number of Senators and Representatives in Congress to which the District would be entitled if it were a State, but in no event more than the least populous State; they shall be in addition to those appointed by the States, but they shall be considered, for the purposes of election of President and Vice President, to be electors appointed by a State; and they shall meet in the District and perform such duties as provided by the twelfth article of amendment.

Section 2. The Congress shall have the power to enforce **this** article by appropriate legislation.

IN OTHER WORDS, D.C. HAS 3 ELECTORAL VOTES.

WHO ALWAYS GO DEMOCRATIC! (NO MATTER WHAT.)

BUT *THREE ELETORAL VOTES DO NOT A DEMOCRACY MAKE...*

WHAT GOOD IS VOTING FOR PRESIDENT IF YOU CAN'T EVEN VOTE FOR A SCHOOLBOARD?

CONGRESS AGREED, AND IN 1968 D.C. WAS ALLOWED TO HAVE A POPULARLY ELECTED SCHOOLBOARD

IN 1973, CONGRESS PASSED THE HOME RULE ACT, GIVING THE DISTRICT POPULARLY ELECTED MAYOR, CITY COUNCIL, AND THE RIGHT TO, AMONG OTHER THINGS, ISSUE LICENCE PLATES & PARKING TICKETS.

LOVE THEM PARKING TICKETS !!!!!

BUT EVEN WITH THIS, AND A **NON-VOTING** CONGRESSMAN (SINCE 1971), IT WASN'T ENOUGH...

TAXATION WITHOUT REPRESENTATION IS TYRANNY!! GIMMIE FULL STATEHOOD RIGHTS NOW!!

UH.. SURE

IN 1978, ANOTHER AMENDMENT PASSED CONGRESS DOING JUST THAT.

THE TWENTY-FOURTH AMENDMENT (1964)

AFTER A MONTH OF SOUTHERN FILIBUSTERING IT FINALLY PASSED THE SENATE.
NOW IT WAS EMANUEL CELLER'S TURN...

IT WAS RATIFIED ON JAN. 23, 1964.

ARTICLE XXIV

Section 1. The right of citizens of the United States to vote in any primary or other election for President or Vice President, for electors for President or Vice President, or for Senator or Representative in Congress, shall not be denied or abridged by the United States or any State by failure to pay any poll tax or other tax.

Section 2. The Congress shall have the power to enforce this article by appropriate legislation.

BUT THIS ONLY COUNTED FOR FEDERAL ELECTIONS. WHAT ABOUT STATE & LOCAL ONES?

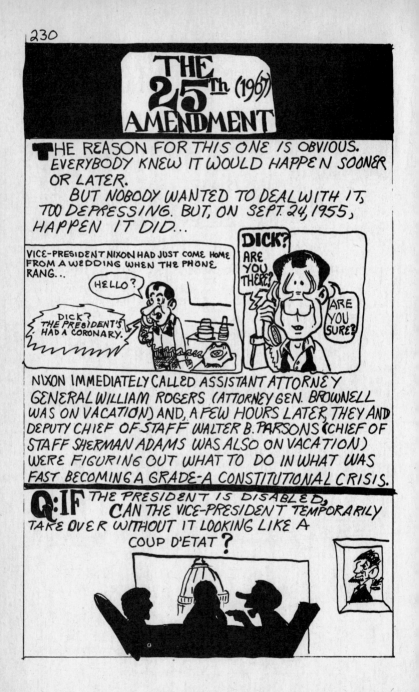

THE 25Th (1967) AMENDMENT

THE REASON FOR *THIS ONE* IS OBVIOUS. EVERYBODY KNEW IT WOULD HAPPEN SOONER OR LATER.

BUT NOBODY WANTED TO DEAL WITH IT, TOO DEPRESSING. BUT, ON SEPT. 24, 1955, HAPPEN IT DID...

VICE-PRESIDENT NIXON HAD JUST COME HOME FROM A WEDDING WHEN THE PHONE RANG...

HELLO?

DICK? THE PRESIDENT'S HAD A CORONARY.

DICK? ARE YOU THERE?

ARE YOU SURE?

NIXON IMMEDIATELY CALLED ASSISTANT ATTORNEY GENERAL WILLIAM ROGERS (ATTORNEY GEN. BROWNELL WAS ON VACATION) AND, A FEW HOURS LATER, THEY AND DEPUTY CHIEF OF STAFF WALTER B. PARSONS (CHIEF OF STAFF SHERMAN ADAMS WAS ALSO ON VACATION) WERE FIGURING OUT WHAT TO DO IN WHAT WAS FAST BECOMING A GRADE-A CONSTITUTIONAL CRISIS.

Q:IF THE PRESIDENT IS DISABLED, CAN THE VICE-PRESIDENT TEMPORARILY TAKE OVER WITHOUT IT LOOKING LIKE A COUP D'ETAT?

MEANWHILE...

SENATORS ESTES KEFAUVER AND KENNETH KEATING WERE PUTTING THE FINISHING TOUCHES ON THE DISABILITY AMENDMENT, CALLED SJ-35

IT WORKS!!

TOOT

BUT, ON AUG. 10, 1963, JUST A FEW WEEKS BEFORE FORMAL DEBATE IN THE SENATE WAS DUE TO START, KEFAUVER DIED. THE WHOLE THING WAS POSTPONED FOR AT LEAST FOUR MONTHS...

THEN, ON NOV. 22...

Z

ON THAT HORRIBLE DAY, WHILE JFK WAS STILL ON THE OPERATING TABLE, THE NATION WAS FORCED TO STARE THE PROBLEM IN THE FACE. WHAT WOULD HAPPEN IF KENNEDY SURVIVED AS A VEGETABLE? THERE WAS A RUMOR L.B.J. HAD JUST HAD A HEART ATTACK. THE NEXT TWO PEOPLE IN LINE WERE 73 AND 88 YEARS OLD, RESPECTIVELY.

BUT KENNEDY DID DIE, AND A SEEMINGLY HEALTHY LYNDON BAINES JOHNSON BECAME PRESIDENT.

L.B.J. AND SPEAKER JOHN McCORMACK (D-MASS) MADE AN AGREEMENT SIMILAR TO THE ONE L.B.J. MADE WITH KENNEDY.

SEN. BIRCH BAYH (D-IND), KEFAUVER'S SUCCSESSOR, AS CHAIRMAN OF THE SUBCOMMITTEE ON THE CONSTITUTION, MADE A MAJOR, IF OBVIOUS, DISCOVERY.

A VICE-PRESIDENT IS NECESSARY AT ALL TIMES.

SO A METHOD OF FILLING VACANCIES IN THE VICE-PRESIDENCY WAS ADDED TO SJ-23, WHICH PASSED THE SENATE IN THE SPRING OF 1964.

AFTER A DELAY OF A YEAR (THE HOUSE
THOUGHT IT IN BAD TASTE UNTIL THERE
WAS A VICE-PRESIDENT) SJ-1, AS IT WAS
NOW CALLED, WAS PASSED OVERWHELMINGLY
ON JULY 6th, 1965.

ON FEB 10, 1967, IT BECAME...

ARTICLE XXV

FOR THE SAKE OF CONTINUITY, WE'LL START WITH §2

Section 2. Whenever there is a vacancy in the office of the Vice President, the President shall nominate a Vice President who shall take office upon confirmation by a majority vote of both Houses of Congress.

THE CASE:

U.S. vs. AGNEW (1973)

FED. REP.

QUESTION:

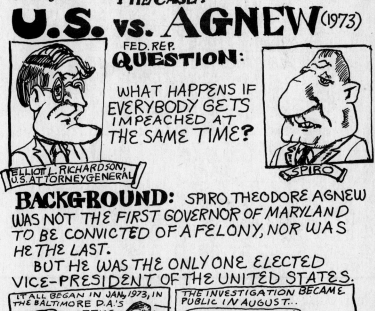

WHAT HAPPENS IF
EVERYBODY GETS
IMPEACHED AT
THE SAME TIME?

ELLIOT L. RICHARDSON,
U.S. ATTORNEY GENERAL

SPIRO

BACKGROUND: SPIRO THEODORE AGNEW
WAS NOT THE FIRST GOVERNOR OF MARYLAND
TO BE CONVICTED OF A FELONY, NOR WAS
HE THE LAST.

BUT HE WAS THE ONLY ONE ELECTED
VICE-PRESIDENT OF THE UNITED STATES.

IT ALL BEGAN IN JAN, 1973, IN
THE BALTIMORE D.A.'S
OFFICE.

I'VE BEEN PAYING OFF
THE VICE-PRESIDENT...

THE INVESTIGATION BECAME
PUBLIC IN AUGUST...

AGNEW'S BEEN
INDICTED
!!!

NO,
HE HASN'T
BUT
JEEZ!

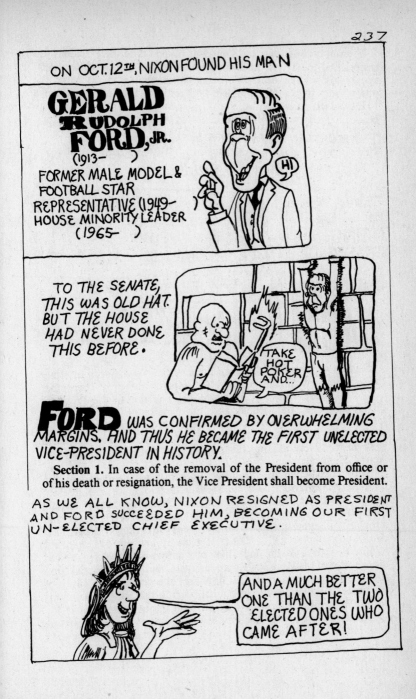

ON OCT. 12TH, NIXON FOUND HIS MAN

GERALD RUDOLPH FORD, JR.

(1913–)

FORMER MALE MODEL & FOOTBALL STAR

REPRESENTATIVE (1949–)

HOUSE MINORITY LEADER (1965–)

HI

TO THE SENATE, THIS WAS OLD HAT. BUT THE HOUSE HAD NEVER DONE THIS BEFORE.

TAKE HOT POKER AND...

FORD WAS CONFIRMED BY OVERWHELMING MARGINS. AND THUS HE BECAME THE FIRST UNELECTED VICE-PRESIDENT IN HISTORY.

Section 1. In case of the removal of the President from office or of his death or resignation, the Vice President shall become President.

AS WE ALL KNOW, NIXON RESIGNED AS PRESIDENT AND FORD SUCCEEDED HIM, BECOMING OUR FIRST UN-ELECTED CHIEF EXECUTIVE.

AND A MUCH BETTER ONE THAN THE TWO ELECTED ONES WHO CAME AFTER!

Section 3. Whenever the President transmits to the President pro tempore of the Senate and the Speaker of the House of Representatives his written declaration that he is unable to discharge the powers and duties of his office, and until he transmits to them a written declaration to the contrary, such powers and duties shall be discharged by the Vice President as Acting President.

THIS SECTION WENT OFF WITHOUT A HITCH IN EARLY JULY, 1985, WHEN PRESIDENT REAGAN HAD A CANCEROUS TUMOR REMOVED.

GEORGE BUSH BECAME ACTING PRESIDENT OF THE UNITED STATES FOR SEVEN WHOLE HOURS.

HEY, DON! WANNA BECOME AMBASSADOR TO IRAN? OR MAYBE MARS, HMM?

FOUR HOURS AND TWENTY MINUTES

Section 4. Whenever the Vice President and a majority of either the principal officers of the executive departments or of such other body as Congress may by law provide, transmit to the President pro tempore of the Senate and the Speaker of the House of Representatives their written declaration that the President is unable to discharge the powers and duties of his office, the Vice President shall immediately assume the powers and duties of the office as Acting President.

Thereafter, when the President transmits to the President pro tempore of the Senate and the Speaker of the House of Representatives his written declaration that no inability exists, he shall resume the powers and duties of his office unless the Vice President and a majority of either the principal officers of the executive department or of such other body as Congress may by law provide, transmit within four days to the President pro tempore of the Senate and the Speaker of the House of Representatives their written declaration that the President is unable to discharge the powers and duties of his office. Thereupon Congress shall decide the issue, assembling within forty-eight hours for that purpose if not in session. If the Congress, within twenty-one days after receipt of the latter written declaration, or, if Congress is not in session, within twenty-one days after Congress is required to assemble, determines by two-thirds vote of both Houses that the President is unable to discharge the powers and duties of his office, the Vice President shall continue to discharge the same as Acting President; otherwise, the President shall resume the powers and duties of his office.

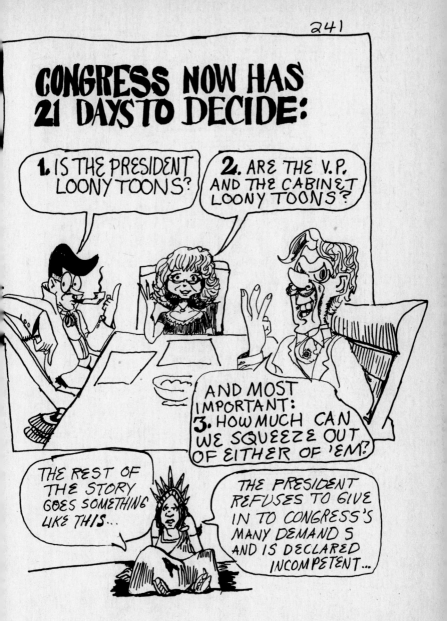

BUT IT WASN'T JENNINGS RANDOLPH OR A CONSTITUTIONAL AMENDMENT THAT GOT 18-YEAR-OLDS THE VOTE...

MAYBE IF WE GAVE THOSE BRATS THE VOTE, THEY'D STOP RIOTING

SO THE 18-YEAR-OLD VOTE WAS PUT IN THE VOTING RIGHTS ACT OF 1970.

AND ON JULY 10th, 1970, JENNINGS RANDOLPH'S CRUSADE TO EXTEND THE FRANCHISE TO THOSE WHO WOULD BE CALLED ON TO DEFEND THE NATION CAME TO A SUCCESSFUL END.

OR DID IT?

LOCAL BOARDS OF ELECTION BEGAN TO PANIC. "JIM CROW" POLLING PLACES MANDATED BY THE SUPREME COURT WERE BOTH DEGRADING AND EXPENSIVE.

AS SOON AS THE NEW CONGRESS WAS SWORN IN, THE RANDOLPH AMENDMENT WAS REVIVED AND WAS INTRODUCED, PASSED AND RATIFIED IN LESS THAN SIX MONTHS—A RECORD!

ARTICLE XXVI

Section 1. The right of citizens of the United States, who are eighteen years of age or older, to vote shall not be denied or abridged by the United States or by any State on account of age.

Section 2. The Congress shall have power to enforce this article by appropriate legislation.

AND HOW DID THESE NEW VOTERS VOTE?

VOTE? I GOT BETTER THINGS TO DO, MAN.

AND THOSE WHO DID, VOTED LIKE THEIR PARENTS.